A

M000318342

Wordsworth Editions

First published in England 1993 by
Wordsworth Editions Ltd
Cumberland House
Crib Street
Ware
Hertfordshire SG12 9ET

ISBN 1 85326 801 1

The editors and publishers have pleasure in
thanking the castle owners and administrators, and the vario
heritage authorities, without whose assistance
this book would not have been possible, and particularly
for their generous response with photographs.

Cover: Neuschwanstein, Bavaria
Opposite: aerial view of Arundel, England

Produced by Aldino Limited
Text conversion and pagination by
August Filmsetting, St Helens, UK
Printed and bound in Italy by Amadeus S.p.A.

Contents

All information supplied is correct at the time of
going to press, but intending visitors should
telephone in advance to check times of opening
and the availability of facilities

*Dirleton Castle, open all year round to
visitors, has three 13th-century
towers to the left of the entrance,
surrounded by a lesser courtyard. The
main entrance had a murder hole, a
guardroom to the right, and a*
4 *portcullis chamber above*

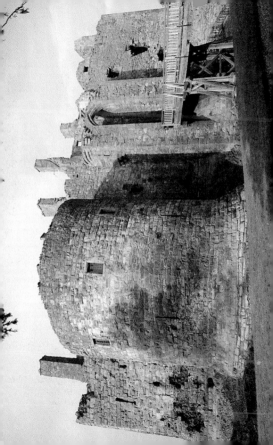

Introduction

As space and entries necessarily are limited, in order for the reader to appreciate the complex strengths and splendors of castle construction, a brief guide follows to the different types of buildings and their features.

Earthwork castles

The very earliest 'castles' were prehistoric, simple fortifications of earth. These were later developed into those built of earth and timber, which likewise have been omitted from this guide. They require the greatest effort on the part of the visitor to imagine what they would have looked like, having suffered through time. Significant detail can only be discovered by archaeological excavation but the role of earthworks in developing fortifications is important in allowing a greater appreciation of castles in general.

The earliest and simplest forms of castle were the ringworks comprising the domestic buildings of the lord's residence, encircled by a ditch. The spoil from this, when piled round the inside edge of the ditch would form a rampart onto which a timber breastwork was built, adding a further 2m (6ft 8in) to the defenses.

The entrance through these defenses was protected by a wooden gatehouse, possibly as much as 5m (16ft 6in) square and 8m (26ft 6in) high, though the very large ringworks had even larger gatehouses. A portcullis would have been worked from the room above the entrance passage, and the drawbridge, a simple moveable wooden bridge spanning the ditch. This basic defense would protect a hall and chamber for the lord, a kitchen, stables, workshop and well, and they continued to be built for several centuries. In order to qualify as castles, Norman ringworks of the later 11th century had to be protected by a ditch at least 3m (10ft) deep.

The next development was of the motte and bailey castles. The motte, a conical mound, would have been built either with rocks and earth quarried from the encircling ditch, or by shaping the sides of a conveniently-sited knoll. These mounds varied greatly in size, as did the buildings placed on them, but they would have carried at least a small tower with limited accommodation. The bailey, built at ground level beside the motte and encircled by the same dry ditch, was also defended by a rampart which was sometimes encased in timber. Ideally kidney-shaped in plan, so that its area could be covered by bow-shot from the motte, the bailey housed most of the domestic buildings, probably comprising a hall for formal use, a kitchen, forge, armory, stables and barns.

Access between the motte and bailey was purposely difficult, and the Bayeux Tapestry depicts 'flying' bridges being used to reach the top of the motte. At other castles, tunnels were dug into the basement of the towers or steep steps cut into the side of the motte.

Keeps

Shell keeps were the next to appear, at the end of the 11th century, replacing wooden palisades on mottes; these stone structures encased the existing motte in stone, usually uncoursed and often undressed. The entrance was usually a simple doorway in the wall, though sometimes a small tower commanded the entrance. Rooms were arranged around the inside of the walls, with a central, usually circular, courtyard.

The success of these stone-built fortresses led to the simple square keep. This was no more than a stone hall, raised to first-floor level and entered at that level via a flight of steps. At ground level, the thick walls featured slit windows. Enlarged by placing a second chamber adjacent to and parallel with the hall, these hall keeps were also plain on the outside but were clearly a development, being two storeys in height with pilaster buttresses added and spiral stairs in each corner. These led from the first-floor entrance up to the battlements and down to the ground-floor.

The tower keep evolved at much the same time. These had a much smaller base area, often as little as 20m² (39.2sq yds), but they rose to three or four storeys in height. The outer walls, much like those of the hall keeps, tended to be decorated by pilaster strips rising from a splayed plinth, which not only had the effect of spreading the load of the walls, but in addition provided protection at ground level against attack by battering rams. The corners of these keeps were usually strengthened by closely-placed pilasters, buttresses or corner turrets, which would then rise above the main roof level.

The roofs themselves were almost flat, and because of the span involved, two parallel roofs were required. The outer walls rose above the roof, serving both as a parapet and as protection against fire arrows. Battlements were also a common feature, as were hoards. Windows were tall and narrow, especially at ground level, and many were arrow-loops.

Entry to tower keeps, in common with virtually all keeps, was generally at first-floor level, approached by stairs built against the outer wall. The entrance to the forebuilding, which projected from the side of the keep and enclosed the stairs, was protected by a door and portcullis with additional protection often being given by the inclusion of a pit halfway up the stairs, crossed by a drawbridge. Occasionally entry to the keep was at second-floor level, so as to provide extra space for the added defenses.

Entering the keep via the stairs and forebuilding, you would have arrived in the hall, which in other tower keeps might have been entered through a small lobby. In the larger tower keeps, this floor would be divided by a crosswall and would contain the stairs to the basement and second floor, latrines and a chapel. The second floor would contain another large hall, private bedchambers and latrines, possibly a second chapel and kitchens, though these would not be elaborate. Heating was by open fires, with the flues rising through the thickness of the walls to the roof. The windows on this upper floor were larger than those below.

A century after the Norman conquest of England, castles had developed as far as the round and polygonal keeps, built from a circular ground plan with large rectangular turrets projecting from the walls to produce a more interesting and complicated layout. Although entrance was still at first-floor level, there was generally no forebuilding. The internal stairs were a single spiral running from the ground floor to the roof, but apart from these apparent differences and the often elaborate layout of the chambers, the floor-by-floor arrangements were similar to those of the square keeps.

10 *The imposing western towers and curtain wall of the Château d'Angers*

Curtain walls

From earliest times, basic protection was provided by walls that enclosed the dwellings, initially built from timber, later from stone. The timber walls were backed by ramparts of earth for additional solidity and protection against battering rams. Later this earthen support would have been completely encased in timber for added support, thus enabling the frontal timbers to project above the earth backing, which itself formed a convenient sentry-walk, to form a breastwork.

The stone walls which succeeded the timber had sufficient mass to withstand battering rams on their own; they also had the advantages of being fireproof and able to accommodate a sentry-walk within their own thickness. The outer facing wall continued beyond the main body of the wall would then form a parapet and if the inner facing wall was also extended, this inner parapet was called a parados.

Thus the essential castle element, the curtain wall, developed. Further additions or embellishments followed; some sentry-walks were covered with lead to protect the masonry from the penetrating rain, and drain holes were also built in, as were holes to carry the beams of a hoard. Parapets became battlemented with crenels (the 'u' in the parapet) and merlons, which continue the parapet between the crenels.

Swing shutters were later added to the crenels for extra security, and from the beginning of the 13th century loop holes were added for the archers in the middle of the merlons, which were themselves surmounted by an overhanging lip to deflect arrows ricocheting off the sides.

Wall towers

The all-important curtain wall defenses linked the wall towers together and although it is not certain when these towers first made their appearance, there is evidence to suggest that a few wooden structures date from earthwork castles; 12th-century examples of wall towers suggest a purely military purpose, having open backs and no accommodation facilities. This changed in the 13th century, when King John rebuilt the wall towers of Dover Castle. These solid stone-based 'D' section towers were closed at the back and had an upper hollow portion which could be used for storage or accommodation. The back of the D faced inwards to the bailey and the rounded side faced outwards. Later towers embodied multi-storey accommodation, usually with short flights of stairs built into the thickness of the walls. These wall towers formed an integral part of the basic structure of the castles throughout the Middle Ages. Curtain walls and towers were often separate entities,

with no access to the tower from the sentry-walk
other than at ground level. Sometimes the
sentry-walk continued round outside the tower,
again without entering the tower, while
occasionally it passed through the tower.

Gatehouses
Every castle had its gatehouse, symbolizing its
character, defenses and power. Although originally there would have been timber gatehouses,
even from excavations it is not possible to judge
accurately their size or construction; but if they
were similar to the early stone constructions,
they would have been square or nearly so.

Some early stone gatehouses had pilaster
buttresses; size obviously varied greatly but
could be up to 15m (50ft) square and two or
three storeys high. The entrance passage to the
gatehouse was defended by a drawbridge,
wooden doors and in most instances by at least
one portcullis. The passage then passed under
the gatehouse, where it was usually further protected by a vault, against fire.

At the end of the 12th century, gatehouses
began to appear with small towers, square or
round, placed on both sides of the gate, and a

*Stauffenberg was originally built in
1233, and the much repaired
battlemented walls and towers are*
still accessible

little later on these towers were joined above the entrance passage, thereby forming a gatehouse with two protecting towers overlooking the approach to the castle. These tower gatehouses provided quite good accommodation and were most usually inhabited by the castle constable. By the early 13th century, gatehouses were often protected by barbicans and drawbridges.

Drawbridges

These fall into four main types, from the simplest gangplank which afforded access across the ditch or moat and which could be very easily retracted, to the only slightly more complex lifting bridges which were hinged on the castle side and raised by chains pulled in from a room above the gatehouse. This simple arrangement provided additional protection, as when raised the bridge formed an additional wooden door.

For larger gate passages requiring longer and heavier drawbridges to span wider ditches, which could not be manually hauled up by pulling on chains, a swing or turning bridge was used. It had the same principle as lifting bridges, but was extended back into the gatehouse and pivoted at its threshold. A counterweight enabled the back of the bridge to swing down

Now beautifully restored and with a military museum, Friedrichstein has commanding views over the Eder

into a pit and the front to rise up, again forming an extra door. The pit into which the back of the bridge swung provided an extra obstacle for the attackers. When down, the bridge was held in place at the back end by a bar, which slid under the counterbalance. When the bridge was raised, a second bar slid across its outer face from an adjacent tower to hold it in position.

By the 14th century, the drawbridge had developed still further, with long beams, counterbalanced on their inner (castle) ends, and pivoted just above the gate opening's threshold. Projecting horizontally from the gatehouse, they had chains affixed to their outer ends which ran down to the outer end corners of the drawbridge. These beams, when swung down by the counterbalances, raised the drawbridge with them. In order to hold the bridge tight against the gate opening, the beams fell back into slots cut into the stonework of the gatehouse. These were called bascula bridges.

Portcullis

This was, in effect, a gate which worked on the principle of sliding down into position from above, guided by grooves cut into the stonework at each side. The portcullis comprised a frame of strong timbers, held together by iron nails. As it

The vast and spectaular Château de

would be needed to drop quickly in an emergency, the lower ends of the vertical timbers were shaped to a point and covered with iron. Although the portcullis timbers formed an open grid, this was stronger than a door, in that it was not hinged and thus it could not be burst open.

The portcullis was raised by a windlass housed in a room immediately above the gate passage, into which the upper part of the portcullis protruded when it was opened up.

Barbicans

These outer fortifications acted as a protection for the main gate, and were often sited on the opposite side of the ditch, astride the approach to the drawbridge. Sizes varied greatly, but their purpose was to delay any attack on the main gate, thereby giving the defenders time to assemble and organize. Some barbicans were joined to the main gatehouse by tall curtain walls on both sides, with both parapets and parados to provide archers not only with the opportunity of firing down onto any attackers who had breached the barbican, but also outwards towards the field.

An aerial view of the beautiful
20 *Austrian Burg Oberranna*

Castle of Hasegg

Tourist Office of Hall, Wallpachgasse 5, 6060 Hall, Tirol, Austria
Telephone: (05223) 6269 or 6220 **fax:** (05223) 622020

Location: from the A12 Innsbrück-Wein road, cross the River Inn at Hall; the Castle, with free parking, is immediately to the right

Opening: all year for guided tours

History: the Castle of Hasegg, with its famous Münzerturm, represents one of the most important landmarks in the Tirol. Records of the Castle date back to 1306, when it was originally built to protect the nearby salt-stores, shipping on the River Inn and the important bridge across it. In 1567, Archduke Ferdinand II had the old Mint transferred from the Castle of Sparberegg to Hasegg, from which the latter gained much popularity and profit, and its minting of silver talers (the precursor of the American dollar) achieved worldwide fame. In 1809, the Mint was closed down and the Castle became increasingly dilapidated; once the largest castle complex in the Inn Valley, it finally succumbed to a huge fire and earthquake and it is now being restored, step by step.

Features: a museum housed in the northern wing provides an insight into Hall's economic and cultural life throughout the centuries

Château d'Hassonville

Château d'Hassonville, 6900 Marche-en-Famenne (Aye) Belgium
Telephone: (084) 31 10 25 **fax:** (084) 31 60 27

Location: 87km (58 miles) SE of Bruxelles, at the junction of the N4 and N35; the Château stands about 4km (2.5 miles) from Marche
Opening: hotel open all year; restaurant closed Monday evening and on Tuesdays
History: Château d'Hassonville was built in 1687 in classical elegance by the governor of March-en-Famenne, expressly for King Louis XIV to have his hunting parties there. It is situated in breathtaking parkland that covers an area extending to over 8,093.56ha (20,000 acres). A student of Lenôtre, who had been responsible for the landscaping of the gardens of Versailles, has also left his undoubted touch of greatness here. Now one of the most prestigious estates in the Belgian Ardennes, this Renaissance castle welcomes the visitor of today, giving the opportunity of discovering the *ambiance* of a castle.
Features: excellent country walks and outdoor pursuits, elegance and comfort and the opportunity to savor the atmosphere of a 300-year-old castle

Alnwick Castle

Alnwick Castle, Alnwick, Northumberland NE66 1NQ, England
Telephone: (0665) 510777 **fax:** 510876

Location: 48km (30 miles) N of Newcastle via A1

Opening: daily from Maundy Thursday (Easter) to mid-October 11.00am to 5.00pm with last admissions at 4.30pm

History: a magnificent border fortress, the second largest inhabited castle in England; it dates back to the 11th century and has been in the possession of the Percys, Earls and Dukes of Northumberland since 1309. Erected by Yvo de Vesey, the first Norman Baron of Alnwick, who became the owner of the town soon after 1066. This mighty stronghold now lies in a peaceful landscape designed by 'Capability' Brown, and was restored to its present splendour by the fourth Duke, between 1854 and 1865.

Features: internal decoration in the classical Italian Renaissance style has replaced the Gothic decoration carried out by Robert Adam in the 18th century. The Castle has some of the finest examples of Italian paintings in the north of England, works by Van Dyck and Turner, an excellent collection of early Meissen porcelain and the regimental museum of the Royal Northumberland Fusiliers in the Abbot's Tower.

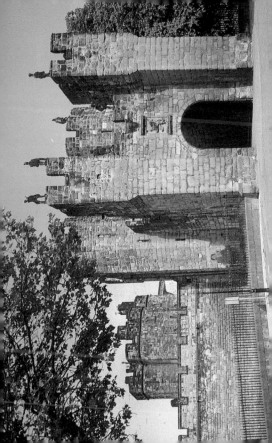

Arundel Castle

Arundel Castle, West Sussex BN18 9AB, England

Telephone: (0903) 883136 **fax:** 884581

Location: 29km (18 miles) W of Brighton via the A27, overlooking the River Arun, 7km (4.3 miles) from the S coast

Opening: from 1 April until last Friday in October, Sunday to Friday from 11.00am to 5.00pm; last admissions 4.00pm

History: built at the end of the 11th century by Roger de Montgomery, Earl of Arundel, this great Castle has been the seat of the Dukes of Norfolk and their ancestors for over 700 years. Extensively damaged in 1643 during the Civil War, when bombarded by the Parliamentary forces, and during their subsequent occupation of it. It was largely rebuilt in the 18th century. Further restoration was carried out late in the 18th century, adding two towers.

Features: rich in art treasures, including works by Van Dyck, Gainsborough and Reynolds; the Barons' Hall is a splendid reproduction medieval hall. The library, built early in the 19th century, measures about 35.66m × 10.667m (117 × 35ft) and is constructed entirely of Honduras mahogany. There are ample car parking facilities, a shop and a restaurant; free-flow tours with guided tours by special arrangement.

Belvoir Castle

Belvoir Castle, Grantham, Lincolnshire NG32 1PD, England
Telephone: (0476) 870262 **fax:** (0476) 870443

Location: 26km (16 miles) E of Nottingham, via A52 from which it is clearly signposted
Opening: from 1 April to 30 September, Tuesday, Wednesday, Thursday and Saturday 11.00am to 5.00pm, plus Sundays in October; other Sundays, Good Friday and bank holiday Monday 11.00am to 6.00pm
History: built by Robert de Todeni, who was standard bearer to William the Conqueror, who gave him the mound on which the Castle now stands, together with all the land visible therefrom. The original building was almost destroyed during the Civil War and rebuilt in 1668, with gardens and plantations added.
Features: magnificent Gobelin tapestries, paintings by Van Dyck, Reynolds, Hogarth, Murillo and one of the finest paintings of Henry VIII by Holbein. The statue gardens are built into the hillside below the Castle. The terraces take their name from the collection of 17th-century sculptures on view by Caius Cibber, sculptor to Charles II. Home of the Duke and Duchess of Rutland; special events include medieval jousting tournaments and concert evenings.

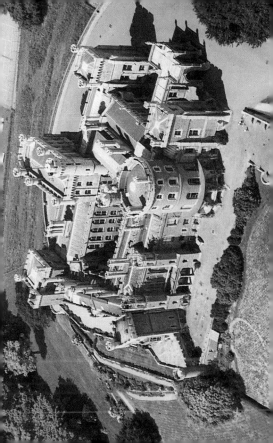

Berkeley Castle

Berkeley Castle, Gloucestershire GL13 9BQ, England
Telephone: (0453) 810332

Location: midway between Bristol and Gloucester, just off the A38 and next to the town of Berkeley

Opening: Tuesday to Sunday April through September, from 2.00pm to 4.30pm, opening at 11.00am Tuesday to Saturday May through September and on bank holidays; last admissions 30 minutes before closing time

History: England's oldest inhabited castle, completed in 1153 at the command of Henry II. A magnificent stately home full of treasures has been created by 24 generations of Berkeleys. In 1215, the West Country barons met there before travelling to Runnymede to force King John to sign *Magna Carta*; in 1327, King Edward II was murdered in the dungeon cell. Berkeley Landing in Virginia, now the oldest working plantation in America, was established by the 38 Berkeley men who sailed from Bristol in 1619 and who held the first Thanksgiving there on 4 December 1619.

Features: paintings by English and Dutch masters; tapestries; furniture, silver and porcelain; a massive keep; dungeon and historic Great Hall, and a butterfly farm.

Castle Howard

Castle Howard, York YO6 7DA, England
Telephone: (065 384) 333 **fax:** (065 384) 462

Location: 24km (15 miles) NE of York, off the
A64
Opening: Daily between 19 March and 31
October, from 11.00am, with last admissions
4.30pm; gardens and grounds are opened at
10.00am
History: designed by Vanbrugh 1664-1726 for
the third Earl of Carlisle, assisted by Hawksmoor
who also designed the mausoleum. Castle
Howard is designed as a series of blocks of different heights with a dome forming the centre of
the design. The Great Hall is impressively built
out of stone.
Features: magnificent rooms filled with fine
collections of pictures, statuary and furniture.
Displays of historical costumes date from the
18th century and are changed every year. There
are over 404.678ha (1,000 acres) of parkland
with lawns, woods, nature walks, a scenic lake,
fountains and a beautiful rose garden. A large
impressive stately home, Castle Howard has
been open to the public from the day it was built
and now has a childrens' adventure playground
in addition to a well-stocked plant centre, restaurants, facilities for the disabled and ample
parking.

Dover Castle

Dover Castle, Dover, Kent CT16 14U, England
Telephone: (0304) 201628 **fax:** 214739

Location: on the E side of Dover, overlooking the town. Coaches from London 105km (65 miles) or by train to Dover Priory station. A mini-bus service operates at weekends between April and September from the town center.
Opening: daily from 10.00am to 6.00pm, closing two hours earlier between 1 October and 31 March; last admissions one hour before closing; closed 24-26 December and 1 January
History: perched high above the famous white cliffs, this vast fortress commands the shortest Channel crossing to continental Europe, earning its name 'The Key to England'. It has the longest recorded history of any major fortress, beginning in the Iron Age and continuing beyond the Second World War. The Romans built a lighthouse here, the Anglo-Saxons a fortified town. Soon after the Battle of Hastings, William the Conqueror increased its defenses, yet much dates from the 12th century, or later. Henry II's great medieval fortress, strengthened in the 13th century, was remodelled by Georgian and Victorian engineers.
Features: Hellfire Corner and the labyrinth of tunnels and Dover's essential role in the Second World War.

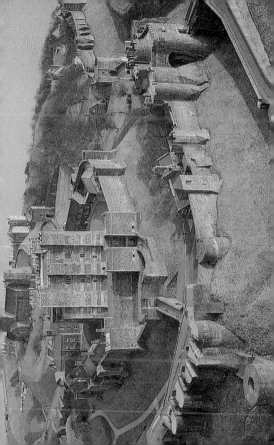

Hedingham Castle

Castle Hedingham, near Halstead, Essex CO9 3DJ, England
Telephone: (0787) 60261 **fax:** (0787) 61473

Location: 40km (24.84 miles) SE of Cambridge, approached along the A604 and B1058; 97km (60 miles) from London
Opening: daily between Easter and the end of October, from 10.00am to 5.00pm
History: one of the finest and best-preserved Norman keeps in England, it was built in 1140 by Aubrey de Vere. The keep walls are 3.657m (12ft) thick at the base, and it is approached by a beautiful Tudor bridge which spans the dry moat surrounding the inner bailey. This was built in 1496 to replace the drawbridge, by the 13th Earl of Oxford, one of Henry VII's chief commanders at the Battle of Bosworth. Home of the de Veres, Earls of Oxford for 550 years, and still owned by their descendant, the Hon Thomas Lindsay; beseiged by King John, and visited by Henry VII, Henry VIII and Elizabeth I.
Features: the banqueting hall, reached from the first floor by a spiral staircase 3.96m (13ft) wide and constructed round a central column, was also the armory and has a splendid minstrels' gallery and a timbered ceiling supported by a magnificent central arch 8.534m (28ft) wide, the largest Norman arch in England.

Hever Castle

Hever, Edenbridge, Kent TN8 7NG, England
Telephone: (0732) 865224 **fax:** 866796

Location: about 38km (23.598 miles) SSE of London and 4.827km (3 miles) SE of Edenbridge, off the B2026 between Sevenoaks and East Grinstead

Opening: 16 March to 7 November, between 12 noon and 6.00pm; gardens open one hour earlier; winter closing one hour earlier

History: the massive gatehouse, outer walls and moat were constructed in 1270. Two hundred years later, the Bullen (or Bolyn) family added a Tudor dwelling house inside the walls. Hever Castle was the childhood home of Anne Bolyn, second wife of Henry VIII and mother of Queen Elizabeth I. The estate was acquired by William Waldorf Astor in 1903, who restored the Castle and built the Tudor Village. The gardens were created between 1904-8.

Features: memories of Anne Bolyn; superb collections of furniture, paintings and *objets d'art*. Spectacular Italian garden containing statuary and sculpture dating from Roman to Renaissance times. The formal gardens include a walled rose garden, fine topiary work and a maze. There is a 14.164ha (35 acre) lake, and there are streams, cascades and fountains. There are restaurants, a gift shop and disabled facilities.

Highclere Castle

Highclere Castle, Highclere, Newbury, Berkshire
RG15 9RN, England
Telephone: (0635) 253210 **fax:** (0635) 254051

Location: 105km (65.2 miles) W of London via M4 motorway and A34, situated 7.25km (4.5 miles) S of Newbury

Opening: Wednesday to Sunday from 2.00pm to 6.00pm during July, August and September, and bank holiday Sundays and Mondays excluding Christmas; last admissions 5.00pm

History: the Castle was the original ancestral seat of the politician fourth Earl of Caernarvon, one of the greatest hosts of Queen Victoria's reign. Regarded as one of the finest creations of Sir Charles Barry, builder of the Houses of Parliament; the parkland and extensive lawns were designed in part by 'Capability' Brown.

Features: richly decorated interiors ranging in style from Church Gothic through Moorish flamboyant and rococo revival. Special exhibition records the exploration of the fifth Earl from Thebes and the Valley of the Kings, while the warren of rooms below stairs presents a fascinating picture of a servant's way of life. There is a walled garden, orangery and yew walk leading to a secret garden. Traditional country tea is served in the housekeeper's room.

Leeds Castle

Leeds Castle, Maidstone, Kent ME17 1PL, England
Telephone: (0622) 765400 **fax:** 735616

Location: 64.36km (40 miles) SE of London via M20 motorway, 6.436km (4 miles) E of Maidstone

Opening: daily with exceptions on the eve of special events, open-air concerts and fireworks display, from 11.00am to 6.00pm; November to February 10.00am to 4.00pm; last admissions one hour before closing

History: one of the most ancient castles in England, it was the site of a manor of the Saxon royal family in the ninth century and named after Led, chief minister of Ethelbert IV, King of Kent in 857. It was first built in stone by Norman barons and is listed in the Domesday Book. It became a royal palace on Edward I's accession and was a royal residence to six of England's medieval queens, and a favorite playground of Henry VIII. It was saved for the nation by Lady Baillie (1900-1974), the last private owner.

Features: the Castle rises from amidst a lake surrounded by 202.339ha (500 acres) of parkland. There is a gate tower with dog collar exhibition; 14th-century barbican and fortified mill; Culpeper garden; aviary; duckery; maze and secret grotto; disabled visitors welcomed.

Lincoln Castle

Lincoln Castle, Castle Hill, Lincoln LN1 3AA, England
Telephone: (0522) 511068 **fax:** 526431

Location: 56km (35 miles) NE of Nottingham, overlooking Lincoln; close to Gothic cathedral
Opening: all year 9.30am to 5.30pm Monday to Saturday and 11.00am to 5.30pm Sunday; during winter months closing is 1 hour 30 minutes earlier; last admissions are 30 minutes before closing
History: during the Middle Ages, Lincoln was one of the richest and largest towns in the realm, and the Castle was built in 1068 on a site in the southwest corner of a Roman fort, which overlooked the Witham valley. The Roman walls were covered with an earth bank, then topped by a wooden stockade which was later replaced by stone walls, towers and gates. The motte, the Castle's strong point, was a great mound of earth surrounded by a ditch. The Castle was besieged several times during the 12th century and in 1644 fell to the Parliamentary forces, since when it assumed a position of law and order with a succession of prison and court buildings.
Features: observatory tower with fine views, unique Victorian prison chapel, wall walk and King John's 1215 *Magna Carta* now on exhibition

Muncaster Castle

Muncaster Castle, Ravenglass, Cumbria CA18 1RQ, England
Telephone: (0229) 717203 **fax:** 717010

Location: 30km (18.63 miles) miles W of Windermere in the Lake District, the Castle is situated 1.609km (1 mile) E of the village of Ravenglass on the A595
Opening: daily except Mondays (bank holidays excepted) from end March to end October from 1.00pm to 4.00pm. The gardens and owl centre open every day from 11.00am to 5.00pm
History: the pele tower stands on Roman foundations, and was extended through the centuries to form the existing Castle. The home since the 13th century of the Pennington family, the Castle was built to protect them from the bloodthirsty border raiders.
Features: a 12.19m (40ft) high octagonal library with 6,000 books; four paintings by Sir Joshua Reynolds adorn the drawing room, with its superb barrelled ceiling, while an exceptional Gainsborough graces the dining room, where the walls are hung with leather. An outstanding collection of 17th and 18th-century furniture and three ghosts; spectacular gardens with outstanding collection of azaleas and rhododendrons; owl centre with 'meet the birds' show March-November. Disabled visitors welcome.

Peckforton Castle

Peckforton Castle, Stone House Lane, Peckforton, Tarporley, Cheshire CW6 9TN, England
Telephone: (0829) 260930 **fax:** (0829) 261230

Location: about 40km (24.84 miles) S of Liverpool, just off the A49 and opposite the ruins of medieval Beeston Castle
Opening: daily from Easter to mid-September from 10.00am to 6.00pm
History: built by John Tollemache, Member of Parliament for Cheshire between 1841 and 1872, the Castle was constructed in stone from a quarry a mile away. The architect was Anthony Salvin, who created a functional Victorian home in the style of a 12th-century castle, which is approached through a forbidding gatehouse with its giant archway and broad battlements.
Features: chapel with hexagonal bell turret; stables; coach house; kitchen and servants' wing, which are grouped around a small courtyard; the Great Hall with high stone vaulted ceiling, ornate carved screen and minstrels' gallery. A unique octagonal dining room rests above a cave-like wine cellar. First opened to the public in 1990, the Castle was the venue in 1991 where Twentieth-Century Fox filmed the production of *Robin Hood*. Ample facilities and activities available.

Ripley Castle

Ripley Castle, Ripley, near Harrogate, North Yorkshire HG3 3AY, England
Telephone: (0423) 770152 **fax:** 771745

Location: 27km (17 miles) N of Leeds and 5.5km (3.5 miles) N of Harrogate via the A61
Opening: May to September 11.30am to 4.30pm Tuesdays to Sunday, plus bank holidays; closing one hour earlier Tuesdays, Wednesdays and Thursdays in May; also open Saturday and Sundays in April and October, 11.30am to 4.30pm
History: Ripley Castle has been the home of the Ingilbys for more than 660 years. The fortified gatehouse dates from the 1450s; the Old Tower, housing the library of over 2,500 books, dates from 1555. In 1603, the future King James I stayed there, prompting the building of the magnificent plaster ceiling in the Tower Room. There is also a Georgian wing, added in 1782/3.
Features: remarkable Knight's Chamber, with original 1555 wood panelling and waggon roof ceiling, Royal Greenwich Armoury and priest's hiding hole made in 1584 but only discovered by accident in 1964. The Castle gardens feature Victorian hothouses, the National Hyacinth Collection and over 80,000 Dutch bulbs. There is also a walled garden and from 1993 a Bird of Prey Sanctuary.

Rockingham Castle

Rockingham Castle, Market Harborough, Leicestershire LE16 8TH, England
Telephone: (0536) 770240 **fax:** (0536) 771692

Location: 40km (25 miles) E of Leicester via the A47 and A6003, the Castle commands a splendid view of five counties

Opening: Easter Sunday to 3 September, Thursdays and Sundays from 1.30pm to 5.30pm and on other days by appointment; throughout the winter groups by appointment; also Tuesdays in August 1.30pm to 5.30pm and on bank holiday Mondays and Tuesdays following

History: built by William the Conqueror on the site of an earlier fortification. It was a royal fortress used by the early kings of England until the 16th century, when it was granted by Henry VIII to Edward Watson, whose descendants still live there. The Castle walls are Norman, although the dominant influence in the building is Tudor.

Features: a fine collection of English 18th, 19th and 20th-century paintings; the Castle stands in 4.856ha (12 acres) of formal and wild gardens which include a 400-year-old elephant hedge and a rose garden which marks the foundations of the old keep. A free guided tour is available for pre-booked parties. Good parking and catering facilities available.

Tamworth Castle

Tamworth Castle, The Holloway, Tamworth, Staffordshire B79 7LR, England
Telephone: (0827) 63563 **fax:** (0827) 52769

Location: 24.135km (15 miles) NE of Birmingham via the A38 and A453; the Castle may be approached on foot from the town center
Opening: daily from 10.00am to 5.30pm, except Sundays, opening at 2.00pm; last admissions 4.30pm; guided tours for pre-booked groups
History: a typical Norman motte and bailey castle thought to date from the 1180s, constructed on the site of a wooden tower on an artificial mound (motte) built shortly after 1066. The surviving stone structure is a polygonal shell-keep with a square tower set into its wall. The enclosure (lower bailey) would have been bordered by a timber palisade with a ditch outside. Numerous additions and alterations have been made over the years, including the 13th-century arched doorway in the north wing, the 15th-century banqueting hall and Tudor warder's lodge.
Features: there are two battlemented wall-walks; the haunted bedroom in the Norman tower — the ghost of St Editha — and the dungeon. Wheelchair access is restricted to the ground floor and courtyard; there is a shop and toilet but no car park.

HM Tower of London

The Tower of London, Tower Hill, London EC3N 4AB
Telephone: (071) 709 0765 **fax:** 480 5350

Location: easy access from Tower Hill Underground, Fenchurch Street British Rail stations, or No 15 bus route; a river service to Westminster operates from Tower Hill Pier next to the Tower
Opening: daily 9.30am to 6.00pm, Sunday opening an hour later; in winter closing an hour earlier; last admissions an hour before closing
History: the White Tower *illustrated* was built by William the Conqueror because he did not trust his new people. Henry I's Bishop of Durham became the first prisoner. It was a garrison, armory and royal palace. Cromwell did away with the palace; the Victorians moved the zoo, established in the 14th century; the Observatory moved out in 1675, the Royal Mint in 1810, and after 1820 it was no longer a prison whose famous inmates had included kings of Scotland, France and England, Lady Jane Grey, Sir Thomas Moore, Princess (Queen) Elizabeth, Sir Walter Raleigh and William Seymore.
Features: the Traitors' Gate; the entrance from the river to the moat, now drained; the Yeoman warders; the famous Tower ravens; the half-timbered Queen's House, the Jewel Home and the site of the execution block.

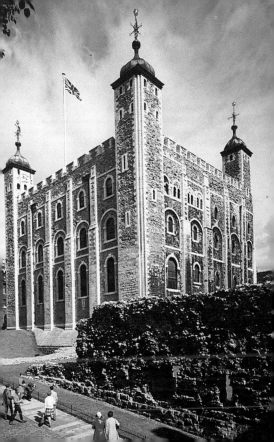

Warwick Castle

Warwick Castle, Warwick, Warwickshire CV34
4QU, England
Telephone: (0296) 495421 **fax:** 401692

Location: on the banks of the River Avon,
12.872km (8 miles) NE of Stratford, the Castle is
easily accessible by car and well signposted
Opening: daily except Christmas Day, 10.00am
to 5.30pm, closing at 4.30pm October to February
History: the finest example of a medieval castle
in England, the site was selected and fortified by
William the Conqueror in 1086. The Castle was
owned by Richard III and for centuries the home
of the Earls of Warwick, including Richard
Neville, 'Warwick the Kingmaker', the first Earl of
Warwick in the 15th century.
Features: the Castle entrance with portcullis;
dungeon and torture chamber; a magnificent
14th-century Great Hall with displays here and
throughout the Castle of over 1,000 pieces of
armor. Six magnificent State Rooms including
the Blue Boudoir, Lady Warwick's boudoir, in
one of 12 rooms featuring a simulated Victorian
houseparty of 1898 arranged by Madame Tuss-
aud's and including a young Winston Churchill
and the future King Edward VII; Oliver Cromwell's death mask; Bonnie Prince Charlie's
shield and the haunted Watergate Tower.

Windsor Castle

Windsor Castle, Windsor, Berks SL4 1NJ, England
Telephone: (0753) 831118; for wheelchair access please phone prior to visit (0753) 868286 **fax:** the Royal Collection (071-839) 8168

Location: 33km (20 miles) W of London via M4 motorway
Opening: subject to change; precincts open daily from 10.00am to 6.15pm; State Apartments from 10.30am to 5.00pm; last admissions 30 minutes before closing
History: the largest inhabited castle in the world, Windsor Castle covers 5.26ha (13 acres). Dating from William the Conqueror, the first stone buildings, including the Round Tower, were erected by Henry II. The defenses we see today are mostly those of Henry III. Edward III was born there. Sir Jaffry Wyatville made tremendous alterations for George IV, providing Windsor with the skyline that we see today. The Castle comprises three parts; the Lower Ward, including St George's Chapel, the Upper Ward in which lie the State Apartments and the Middle Ward, open to the public and including the Round Tower.
Features: the Queen's Presents, Royal Carriages and Queen Mary's Dolls House.

Angers

Château d'Angers, 49100 Angers, France
Telephone: 41 87 43 47 **fax:** 41 87 17 50

Location: 250km (155.25 miles) SW of Paris,
via the N23 motorway at the junction with the
D107, standing beside the river and motorway
Opening: daily from 16 April to 31 May from
9.00am to 12.30pm and from 2.00 to 6.30pm;
from 1 June to 15 September from 9.00am to
7.00pm; from 16 September to 15 April from
9.30am to 12.30pm and from 2.00 to 6.00pm
History: confiscated by Philip Augustus from
John 'the landless', son of Henry II, in 1203. The
Anjou region was part of the royal estates in
1230, when Louis I started work on the present
Castle on the site of the former fortress of Foulques. It forms a pentagon some 660m (2,165ft)
across surrounded, except on the side overlooking the river, by 17 cylindrical towers, each
40-60m (131-197ft) high. In the 15th century,
Louis II and Yolande d'Aragon built the chapel
and completed the royal residence. Their son,
King René, added the gatehouse, its two towers
and the northern gallery. The roofing and two
upper storeys of each tower were removed by
order of Henry III in 1585, making the towers the
same height as the curtain wall.
Features: the Apocalypse tapestry, created in
1375 for Louis I of Anjou

Brissac

Château de Brissac, 49320 Brissac, France
Telephone: 41 91 22 21 **fax:** 41 91 25 60

Location: 15km (10 miles) S of Angers along
the D761 road in the direction of Poitiers
Opening: daily except Tuesdays from 1 April to
30 June and from 1 September to 3 November
from 9.30 to 11.30am and from 2.15 to 5.15pm;
from 1 July to 31 August daily from 9.30am to
5.45pm; guided tour lasts 45 minutes
History: this imposing building, equally a fortress and a palace, with 150 rooms situated on
seven floors, has been the birthplace of the
Cossé-Brissac line since 1502, and is today the
home of the Marquis and Marquise de Brissac.
One of the tallest châteaux in France, and an
astonishing piece of architecture built on an
enormous scale, it boasts an impressive trium-
phal façade built at the beginning of the 17th
century by Charles II de Cossé, the first Duke of
the line. The medieval towers of the original fortress still remain.
Features: painted and gilded ceilings lit by
crystal chandeliers from Venice and Bohemia;
walls lined with antique tapestries from Flan-
ders, Brussels and Gobelins; the Castle's own
theatre, with the original 19th-century carved
wooden pillars, stage sets and decoration, seat-
ing 200; estate wines tasting cellar

Montreuil-Bellay

Château de Montreuil-Bellay, Montreuil-Bellay
49260, France
Telephone: 41 52 33 06

Location: 60km (40 miles) SE of Angers, on the
N761 road at the junction with the N138
Opening: from Wednesday to Monday from 1
April to 1 November from 10.00am to 12 noon
and from 2.00 to 6.00pm
History: built in 1025 by Foulques Nerra, and in
turn beleaguered by the Plantagenets, the Kings
of England and the Kings of France; traces of the
Château's origins still remain. More prosperous
and comfortable times have also left their mark;
the seigneurs of Mélun-Tancarville and Harcourt
added elegant buildings of the 15th and 16th
centuries; the New Castle; Collegiate Church;
Canon's House; the Sweating Rooms (or Hot
Baths) and the Oratory, with frescoes of musi-
cian angels built for Yolande of Laval.
Features: 17th and 18th-century furniture in
the sitting rooms; the Duchess of Longueville's
bedroom, with Renaissance furnishings; medieval kitchen, with central fireplace; arched
underground passages; barbican, moat and fortified ramparts; the second drawbridge, flanked
by cylindrical towers with a smaller square tower
set off to the right; also the main courtyard of the
new Château, with its 15th-century steps

Montsoreau

Château de Montsoreau, 49730 Montsoreau,
France
Telephone: 41 51 70 25

Location: 70km (46 miles) E of Angers, along
the River Loire via the D952 from Angers, crossing the river to Saumur and continuing to follow
the river in the direction of Chinon
Opening: daily except Tuesdays, All Saints'
Day, Christmas Day and 1 January, from
10.00am to 12 noon and 2.00 to 6.00pm; also
closed on occasions for repairs
History: Montsoreau was built ten years earlier
than the fortress at Langeais, and as such served
as the architectural inspiration for the latter,
where many details such as the parapets, crenellations, window designs and staircase turrets
were duplicated. Originally planned as a square
surrounding a central courtyard, unfortunately
only the main building which faces the Loire was
completed, together with a small part of an
adjoining wing. The façade, which is framed
between two square corner towers, is an
imposing military structure, broken by two vertical rows of mullioned windows surmounted by
double gable windows and topped by pinnacles
which emerge from the lower part of the roof
level with the covered walkway and parapet.
Features: the Koumia Museum

le Plessis-Bourré

Château du Plessis-Bourré, 49460 Ecuillé, France
Telephone: 41 32 06 01 **fax:** 41 32 06 72

Location: from Angers via D107 N 15km (10 miles) to Sablé, just S of the D74 junction
Opening: daily from 1 July to 31 August from 10.00am to 6.00pm; from 16 February to 30 June and 1 September to 15 November, except Wednesdays and Thursday mornings, from 10.00am to 12 noon and from 2.00 to 6.00pm; and from 26 December to 15 February except Wednesdays from 2.00 to 6.00pm
History: a 15th-century fortress set in a vast expanse of water, as when first built in 1468. Designed by Jean Bourré, state treasurer and friend of Louis XI, it is square in plan with four wings on imitation brayes. The highest of the cylindrical corner towers forms the keep with a parapet and covered sentry-walk, topped by another level set back from the rim, surmounted by a pepperpot turret. The most imposing of the mullioned windows of the principal residence show three superimposed rows, predating early Renaissance style.
Features: moat crossed by a 44m (144ft) bridge and double drawbridge; guardroom interior's original 24 compartments with allegorical or decorative paintings; 15th-century furniture.

Saumur Castle

Château de Saumur XIV, 49400 Saumur, France
Telephone: 41 51 30 46 **fax:** 41 67 45 65

Location: 250km (155.25 miles) SW of Paris
by A11 motorway to Angers, Saumur is 45km
(27.95 miles) SE along the Loire valley on the
D952 in Anjou, offering splendid views
Opening: daily from 15 June to 15 September
from 9.00am to 7.00pm, guided tours in English,
an average tour lasts 60 minutes; from 16 to 30
September and from 1 April to 14 June from
9.00am to 12 noon and from 2.00 to 6.00pm;
from 1 October to 31 March from 10.00am to 12
noon and from 2.00 to 5.00pm, closed on
Tuesdays
History: rebuilt about 1360 by Louis I, Duke of
Anjou, on the foundations of St Louis' fortress,
the castle of Saumur during the 15th century
was the epitome of a fairytale castle. Used as a
Protestant stronghold during the 17th century,
as a prison during the 18th century and a barracks during the 19th century, the Castle became
a museum during the 20th century.
Features: bridgehead, between two pepperpot
turrets, but no drawbridge; guardroom with
original fireplace; porch with portcullis; a 200m
(656ft) deep well in the courtyard and 13th-
century winch; watchtower; dungeon; Museum
of Decorative Arts, and Museum of the Horse.

Sully-sur-Loire

Château de Sully, 45600 Sully-sur-Loire, France
Telephone: 38 36 25 60

Location: 140km (93 miles) S of Paris via the
A10 motorway, or *route national* 20 to Orléans
then by the N60 via Châteauneuf, about 45km
(30 miles)
Opening: daily from 1 March to 30 November
from 9.00am to 12 noon and from 2.00 to
6.00pm
History: built in the tenth century commanding
a historic Loire crossing point, controlling the
passage between two territories, Forêt d'Orléans
and Sologne, the Castle was designed and decorated by Maximilian de Béthune, better known
as Sully, Henry IV's financial secretary. Rectangular, with mighty curtain walls linking its four
tapered round towers, battlements and turrets,
Sully still possesses its original steeply-pitched
roof between two gables. In the 16th century,
the Renaissance wing or little castle was added
by the Lords of la Tremoille, who had taken over
ownership of the Castle in the 14th century. Further rebuilding took place in the 17th century.
Since 1962, the Château has been in the charge
of the Department of the Loiret.
Features: timber framing under the highest
room in the Castle, dating from 1363, and the
keep; the Château is floodlit every night.

Auerbach Castle

Auerbacher Schloss, 6140 Bensheim, 3-Auerbach, Germany
Telephone: (06251) 72923 **fax:** 78410

Location: S of Darmstadt, on the Bergstrasse B3 road approach from Ernst-Ludwig-Promenade; the Castle sits above the health resort of Bensheim-Auerbach, 350m (1;148ft) above sea level

Opening: Castle and restaurant open daily from 1 February to 23 December

History: probably built at the beginning of the 13th century by Count von Katzeneinbogen, Auerbach Castle was completely renovated in the 14th century, further altered in the 15th century and left to Hesse in 1479. It was destroyed in the Thirty Years War and fell into decay until restored in 1850 under Grand Duke Ludwig III. It is the most significant ancient monument of the Bergstrasse. The ground plan was for a castle forming an equilateral triangle and today two high round towers still stand, together with the wall surrounding the main building and castle offices. There is a well in the courtyard 62m (203ft) deep, and the northern tower has been made into a viewing tower reached via the bastion and the ramparts.

Features: banquets by arrangement, and summer festivals

Frankenstein Castle

Burg Frankenstein, 6109 Mühital Nieder-
Beerbach, Germany
Telephone: (06151) 54618

Location: from the Darmstadt-Heidelberg
Autobahn exit at Darmstadt-Eberstadt; the
Castle is very close
Opening: the hotel is a new building within the
outer courtyard of the old castle, and open all
year round; restaurant closed on Mondays
History: first mentioned in 1252, but probably
built about 300 years earlier. In the 14th century
the Frankenstein family divided, but the Castle
was extended by the outer bailey. Continuously
in dispute with Hesse, the Castle was finally sold
to them in 1662, and subsequently used as a disabled soldiers' home, a refuge from Louis XIV
and a military prison, before falling into decay. In
1765, a forester's home was constructed on the
foundations and restoration work began under
Ludwig III in the 19th century. Today, a well-
preserved accommodation tower in the central
building exists with a viewing platform on the
ruins of a former residential building, the high
gate tower and shell tower in the defensive wall
of the outer bailey and a small 16th-century
chapel in the outer courtyard.
Features: the legend of St George and the
Dragon

Hohenstein Castle

Burggaststätte 'Waffenschmiede', 6209 Hohenstein 2, Burgruine, Germany
Telephone: (061) 20 33 57 **fax:** (061) 20 63 30

Location: from the Wiesbaden-Köln Autobahn exit Wiesbaden or Frankfurt-Köln Autobahn, exit Idstein; the village of Hohenstein is on a side road off the B54
Opening: the hotel is open from mid-February to the end of December
History: originally built into the cliffs, which form part of the walls which in other parts are 2.5m (8ft) thick; Hohenstein was a massive but simple castle, now in ruins. The hexagonal keep and the walls are open to visitors, and afford beautiful views of the Taunus heights and Aar Valley. The Castle was first mentioned in 1190, and was built by the Counts of Katzeneinbogen. The central castle has a triangular plan, with an inner defensive wall added in the 13th century, with 14th-century extension. There were office buildings in the outer court, destroyed along with the outer defensive wall in the Thirty Years War. The Castle has been in ruins since the 17th century.
Features: summer theatre in the ruins; the hotel is within the castle and has eight rooms and a terraced restaurant

Sababurg Castle

Familie Koseck, Burghotel Sababurg, 3520 Hofgeismar Sababurg, Germany
Telephone: (05671) 8080 **fax:** 808 200

Location: from the Dortmund-Kessel Autobahn exit at Warburg or Breuna, following the signs to Hofgeismar, then Sababurg; or from the Würzburg-Frankfurt-Kassel-Hannover Autobahn, exit at Hann and follow signs to Münden Reinhardshagen and then Sababurg
Opening: from mid-February to mid-January
History: Sleeping Beauty's Castle, built by the Archbishop of Mainz in 1334, in the middle of the Forest of Reinhard. Originally called Zappenburg or Zapfenburg Castle, and in Hessian ownership from 1429, in 1490 it was converted to a hunting lodge. Landgrave Wilhelm IV established a wildlife park in 1571, and it was enclosed by a high wall in 1589; the walled garden still exists. The Castle was laid waste by Imperial forces in 1628, partially demolished in 1862, then fell into decay. A ruin with two domed roofed towers, deep vaulted cellars and, inside, the original fireplaces, and surrounded by a high wall, it was opened as a hotel in 1959.
Features: the extensive zoological park is one of the oldest in Europe; the Castle's relationship with its setting is seen in the use of the names of animals, to identify the hotel rooms.

Schnellenberg Fortress

Burg Schnellenberg, 5952 Altendorn/
Biggessee, Germany
Telephone: (02722) 6940 **fax:** 69469

Location: 120km (80 miles) N of Frankfurt and
75km (50 miles) SE of Dortmund via the A45
Frankfurt-Dortmund road at Olpe; follow signs
to Altendorn
Opening: the hotel is open throughout the year
except for 22-29 December
History: Engelbert von Berg, Archbishop of
Köln, fortified the area and built the Castle in
1222. Fortifications were increased in 1291. The
Castle was purchased by von Fürstenberg, High
Bailiff of the Electorate of Köln, in 1594. The
inside of the lower castle was destroyed by fire in
1899, its south wing now forming the
guesthouse and hotel. The fortress consists of
two parts; the upper fortress, with its irregular
floor plan, and a lower fortress with a long side
wing and magnificent four storey pavilion tower
on the west corner. The main entrance, with its
wide façade, faces the lower fortress.
Features: the remains of a magnificent fireplace
dating from Caspar von Fürstenberg's days;
meticulous renovation work since 1949 has
resulted in returning this beautiful castle to its
former glory, including a museum in what were
the royal stables of the castle.

Schönburg Castle

Familie Hütti, 6532 Oberwesel/Rhien, Germany
Telephone: (06744) 7027 **fax:** (06744) 1613

Location: from the A61 Autobahn to the left of
the Rhien, exit at Laudert/Oberwesel; the Castle
is on a small hill overlooking Oberwesel town
Opening: the Castle is now an hotel/restaurant
History: probably first built in the tenth century,
and once described by Victor Hugo as 'one of the
most venerable hills of rubble of all Europe'.
There is a reference in 1166 to an old tower
(possibly the northern tower, in ruins since
1880), a new tower (possibly the massive gate
tower which still remains) and a tower under
construction. In the 14th century the Castle was
cohereditary, home to three families, with up to
250 inhabitants sharing well equipped accom-
modations. In March 1689, the town of Oberwesel was fired by 1,600 French soldiers billeted
there, destroying the hospital, the town hall, the
Schönburg manor, and 117 houses. At the same
time, Friedrich von Schönburg was killed fight-
ing for the English at the Battle of the Boyne. The
Castle remained a ruin for two centuries. Rebuilding was started in the early 20th century by an
American, Mr Rhinelander. His son sold the
newly-restored Castle to the town council of
Oberwesel.
Features: the collar wall with five battlements

Weilburg Castle

Verwaltung der Stoatlichen, Schlösser und Gärten, AST Schloss-und-Schlossgarten Weilburg, Schlossplatz 3, 35781 Weilburg, Germany
Telephone: (06471) 2236 **fax:** (06471) 1806

Location: from Koblenz E on the B49 via Limburg, crossing the A3 Köln-Frankfurt road; then Weilburg is a further 22km (14 miles)

Opening: daily from March to October from 10.00am to 4.00pm, and from November to February from 10.00am to 3.00pm; the Museum is by guided tour only, last tour one hour before closing, and is closed on Mondays; the grounds are open daily from 9.00am to dusk

History: the residence of the Counts and Dukes of Nassau-Weilburg from 1355-1816. A quadrangular main building, a number of imposing baroque buildings and their magnificent terraced gardens were constructed on the model of Versailles at the beginning of the 18th century. In 1866, the Duchy of Nassau was annexed by Prussia and in 1890 Weilburg Castle became the possession of Luxemburg. From 1945 it has belonged to the State of Nassau.

Features: the Castle courtyard; summer concert festival; the stables, now housing the 'Stadthalle Alte Reitschule'; Weilburg's theatre and concert centre and the Schlosshotel Weilburg

Ashtown Castle

Ashtown Castle, Phoenix Park, Dublin, Ireland
Telephone: (01) 770095 **fax:** (01) 821 3021

Location: the magnificent Phoenix Park comprises 708.99ha (1,752 acres) in Dublin

Opening: from March to May and in October from 10.00am to 1.00pm and from 2.00pm to 5.00pm; from June to September from 9.30am to 6.30pm

History: the original castle may have been built prior to 1600, but definitely existed in the early 17th century, being owned by John Connell in 1641. The estate then extended to some 80.94ha (200 acres). In 1663, the Duke of Ormond bought the lands and Castle to enlarge Phoenix Park to its present size. Ashtown Castle became the residence of the Keeper of the Park. Extensive alterations to the Castle took place in both the 18th and 19th centuries, with the insertion of Georgian windows, new floors and new roofs. Excavation work began in 1989 when clues as to the original form and date of the Castle were revealed. Oak roof timbers were dated by dendrochronology, portions of fireplaces, window jambs, and corbels which carried the floors were all uncovered.

Features: numerous exhibitions, including Phoenix Park Through the Ages; the largest enclosed urban park in western Europe

Aughnanure Castle

Aughnanure Castle, Oughterard, Co Galway, Ireland
Telephone: (091) 82214

Location: some 3km (2 miles) S of Oughterard, near the shore of Lough Comb
Opening: daily from mid-June to mid-September, from 9.30am to 6.30pm; last admissions 5.50pm
History: the Castle, which stands on a rocky island, is a well-preserved example of an Irish tower house. The ground plan is nearly square, with an extension at the northwest corner, where the Drimneen River helps form a natural defense. The Castle was a stronghold of the O'Flaherty clan between the 14th and 16th centuries. The original castle on the site possibly dated from 1256. The tower rises from a battered inclined base to parapets which are crenellated in the Irish manner. The entrance is defended internally by a gun loop and murder hole. Inside the door there is a guard's cubicle to the right, and a stone spiral stair rising to the upper apartments to the left. The ground floor was used as a storeroom. The upper floor, with wide mullioned windows, was normally the general living room.
Features: remarkable caverns under the rocks on which the Castle and its approaches stand

Ayesha Castle

Ayesha, Killiney, Co Dublin, Ireland
Telephone: (01) 285 2323

Location: just below Killiney village, through Gothic archways, 11.3km (7 miles) from Dublin on the Victoria road

Opening: during March from 10.00am to 2.00pm, April and May from 2.00 to 5.00pm on Tuesdays and Thursdays; June and July from 11.00am to 3.00pm on weekends only

History: a romantic 19th-century Victorian castle of ashlar features a round tower with various turrets which afford the finest views over Killiney Bay and Sugar Loaf. Originally named Victoria Castle to commemorate the accession of Queen Victoria, it was built by Robert Warren but gutted by fire in 1924. In 1928, Sir Thomas Power purchased the Castle, restoring it and renaming it Ayesha after the goddess in Rider Haggard's book *She*. In 1947, it was purchased by Colonel Aylmer and the Castle has remained in the family since.

Features: most notably these include the fine oak panelling in the entrance hall and dining room, together with a magnificent oak spiral staircase. Ayesha Castle is surrounded by 1.82ha (4.5 acres) of gardens and woodland, planted out with an amazing variety of exotic plants, flowers and shrubs.

Blarney Castle

Blarney Castle, Blarney, Co Cork, Ireland
Telephone: (021) 385252 **fax:** (021) 381518

Location: 7km (4.35 miles) from Cork City, off the main N20 Cork-Mallow road

Opening: daily throughout the year, except 24 and 25 December; May and September from Monday to Saturday from 9.00am to 6.00pm; from June to August from 9.00am to 7.00pm; from October to April from 9.00am to 5.00pm or sundown; Sundays from 9.20am to 5.30pm during the summer and from 9.30am to sundown during the winter months

History: the existing castle tower was added to in 1446 by Cormac MacCarthy, and the massive four-storey keep changed hands during the Civil and Williamite Wars and at one point was employed as a prison for the Protestants of Cork. It was Dermot MacCarthy who was gifted with the soft talking flattery known as *plamas* in Ireland; he tried to talk his way out of handing over the Castle to an agent of Queen Elizabeth I. He prevaricated until the Queen declared 'I will have no more of this Blarney talk' and gave the English language a new word.

Features: the Blarney stone, which you should kiss to be endowed the 'gift of the gab', is situated high up on the Castle parapets

Bunratty Castle

Bunratty Castle, Bunratty, Co Clare, Ireland
Telephone: (061) 361511

Location: on the Limerick-Ennis road
Opening: daily except Good Friday and 23-27 December, from 9.30am; last admissions 4.45pm; Folk Park open until 7.00pm June to August, last admissions 6.15pm
History: the great square keep was built in about 1450 by the MacNamaras on the site of several earlier castles. It later fell into the hands of the O'Briens, Princes of Thomond, and was later occupied by Admiral Penn, father of William Penn who gave his name to Pennsylvania. The restored Castle provides a wonderful insight into 15th and 16th-century lifestyles, where Lord Gort's magnificent medieval collection furnishes the private chambers and public offices and the great hall where the Earls of Thomond held court. Once regarded as the strongest castle in Munster, the walls of Bunratty Castle feature three 'murder holes', which allowed the defenders to pour boiling water on the attackers below.
Features: the nearby Folk Park recalls the 19th-century lifestyle of the Shannon farming community, with displays of bread and candle making, thatching and flour milling

Cahir Castle

Cahir Castle, Cahir, Co Tipperary, Ireland
Telephone: (052) 41011

Location: sited on a rocky island in the River Suir, beside the main road from Dublin to Cork

Opening: daily from April to mid-June and mid-September to October from 10.00am to 6.00pm; mid-June to mid-September from 9.00am to 7.30pm; and November to March from 10.00am to 1.00pm and from 2.00pm to 4.30pm; last admissions 40 minutes before closing

History: one of the largest and best-preserved castles in Ireland, but the time of its first fortification is unknown. In 1375, the Barony of Cahir was granted to James of Ormond and to Elizabeth his wife. Most of what remains belongs to the 15th and 16th centuries, the work of successive descendants of James of Ormond. The estates of the Earl of Glengall passed through the Encumbered Estates Court in 1853, and he himself died in 1858. His daughter and her son lived in Cahir Castle until it was taken into State care as a national monument in 1964.

Features: the keep and the towers of the inner ward and the barbican towers have been reroofed using trusses of native oak and natural slates. New oak floors have been fitted, including that of the prison tower.

Castle Matrix

Castle Matrix, Rathkeale, Co Limerick, Ireland
Telephone: (069) 64284

Location: 28km (17.39 miles) from Limerick on the main road to Killarney

Opening: from 15 May to 15 September from Saturday to Tuesday from 1.00pm to 5.00pm, or at other times by prior arrangement

History: the square fortress was built in about 1440 by the seventh Earl of Desmond, who was one of the earliest Normans to write poetry in Irish. This poetic connection was continued in Robert Southwell, the metaphysical poet whose family was granted the Castle after the Desmond rebellion. The Castle takes its name from the sanctuary of Matres, the Celtic goddess of love and poetry, on which the Castle stands. Further poetic connections exist; in 1580 the Elizabethan poets Edmund Spenser and Captain Walter Raleigh first met there, and the Castle is thought to have provided the inspiration for Spenser's famous poem *The Faerie Queen*. Castle Matrix has been restored by its new owner, Colonel Sean O'Driscoll, and is the home of the Heraldry Society of Ireland.

Features: a collection of manuscripts housed in the library dating back to Elizabethan times includes records of the 'Wild Geese', who fled Ireland in 1607 to serve in France and Spain

Charleville Forest Castle

Charleville Forest Castle, Tullamore, Co Offaly, Ireland
Telephone: (0506) 21279

Location: situated about 1km (0.66 mile) S of the center of Tullamore

Opening: from April to May, on Saturdays, Sundays and bank holidays from 2.00 to 5.00pm; from June to September Wednesday to Sunday and bank holidays from 11.00am to 5.00pm, and by appointment only from October to March

History: Charleville Forest Castle is the finest and most spectacular early 19th-century castle in Ireland, and the Gothic masterpiece of Francis Johnson who designed it in 1798. Planned by Lord Tullamore, it took 12 years to complete, and although in need of considerable repair to the stable buildings and chapel, the restoration work is in hand under the guidance of the present owners, the Vance, Heavey-Alagna family. The gallery which runs the entire length of the garden wall is considered to be one of the finest Gothic Revival rooms in the country. On either side of the great stairway are the huge drawing room and dining room, and the library which leads to the chapel through a hidden doorway.

Features: unfortunately there is no real access for wheelchairs

Donegal Castle

Donegal Castle, Donegal Town, Co Donegal, Ireland
Telephone: (073) 22405

Location: built beside the River Eske on a rock at the western end of the town
Opening: currently closed for restoration work
History: a castle or dun was built on the site as early as the 12th century by the O'Donnells, but this was burnt in 1159 by Murtogh McLoughlin. Hugh Roe O'Donnell erected a new castle in 1474, and in 1611 this was granted to Captain Basil Brooke. Brooke had gone to Ireland in 1598 with the English Army, fought in Munster and was appointed a servitor of the Ulster Plantation. During the rebellion of 1641, Donegal Castle was held by Sir Basil's heir, Henry Brooke, though Clanrickarde took it for a short period in 1651. Henry Brooke subsequently resided there. It fell into decay in the 18th century and the owner, the Earl of Arran, placed the Castle in the guardianship of the Office of Public Works in 1898.
Features: the remains consist of a large tower house, a manor house of Jacobean style, a gatehouse and parts of the walls of the courtyard; Donegal Castle is one of the most interesting and picturesque castles in Ireland.

Drimnagh Castle

Drimnagh Castle, Longmile Road, Dublin 12, Ireland
Telephone: (01-280) 2203

Location: in Dublin's suburbs, about 4.5km (3 miles) SW of Dublin city center
Opening: Wednesdays, Saturdays and Sundays from 10.00am to 5.00pm from 15 April to October
History: an outstanding example of an old feudal stronghold, it was, until 1954, one of the oldest continuously-inhabited castles in Ireland and is the only Irish castle still to be surrounded by a flooded moat. This is well stocked with fish, in addition to being a very picturesque feature. The Castle is built from local grey limestone and consists of a great hall, which has been restored, and medieval undercroft, a tall battlemented tower with lookout posts, together with separate outbuildings including stables, dairy, folly tower and old coach house. Restoration work is still in hand.
Features: one of the most attractive features of Drimnagh Castle are the formal gardens, laid out in the 17th century with box hedges, yews, mop-head laurels and an alley of hornbeam, and a collection of up to 20 species of fowl which inhabit the moated area.

Dublin Castle

Dublin Castle, Dame Street, Dublin 2, Ireland
Telephone: (01) 777129 **fax:** (01) 679 7871

Location: built within the original city walls of Dublin, the Castle occupies the southeast corner of the city
Opening: daily except December 24 and 25 and Good Friday, Monday to Friday from 10.00am to 12.15pm and from 2.00 to 5.00pm; on Saturdays, Sundays and public holidays from 2.00 to 5.00pm
History: the Castle was originally built in the 13th century on a site previously settled by the Vikings. It functioned as a military fortress, a prison, treasury, courts of law and the seat of the English Administration in Ireland for 700 years. It was rebuilt in the 17th, 18th, 19th and 20th centuries, and Dublin Castle is now used for important State receptions and presidential inaugurations.
Features: the Castle buildings are comprised of the Upper Yard, which roughly marks the extent of the original 13th-century fortress; the genealogical office built in the 1750-1760 period which contains the Heraldic Museum; the State Apartments; the Cross Block, which separates the Upper and Lower Yards and was first built in 1716; the Round Tower, the Church of the Most Holy Trinity and the former guardroom

Glin Castle

Glin Castle, Glin, County Limerick, Ireland
Telephone: (068) 34173 **fax:** (068) 34364

Location: on the Foynes-Tarbert road, 9km (5.6 miles) W of Foynes and 5km (3 miles) E of Tarbert and the car ferry
Opening: from 10.00am to 12 noon and from 2.00 to 4.00pm during May; group tours by arrangement at other times
History: the 1785 Georgian house became Glin Castle in the 1820s, when the 25th Knight, known as the Knight of the Women, added crenellations and Gothic details. The Castle stands in the middle of a wooded demesne on the banks of the River Shannon. Home of the Fitz-Gerralds for 700 years, the Castle was obviously built with entertaining in mind, with a neo-classical hall featuring elaborate plasterwork and ceiling painted in the original red and green, opening into a grand double staircase with a 'flying ramp'. An 18th-century bookcase in the library has a secret door leading to the hall. The walls throughout the Castle are adorned with portraits, and the dining room windows catch the setting sun, reflected in the river.
Features: the main block of the Castle is available, fully staffed, for occasional lets, sleeping eight people. There is a pleasant walled garden and grounds surround the Castle.

Johnstown Castle

Johnstown Castle, Murrintown, Co Wexford, Ireland
Telephone: (053) 42888 **fax:** (053) 42004

Location: from Dublin via N11, Cork via N25 or Rosslare take the Wexford bypass from which the Castle is clearly signposted

Opening: grounds open all year; Agricultural Museum from June to August, Monday to Friday from 9.00am to 5.00pm, Saturdays and Sundays from 2.00 to 5.00pm; April, May and September until 11 November, Monday to Friday from 9.00am to 12.30pm and Saturdays and Sundays from 2.00 to 5.00pm; 12 November to 31 March Monday to Friday from 9.00am to 12.30pm and from 1.30 to 5.00pm

History: built in 1840, this Gothic Revival castle stands in a lush setting of ornamental trees and shrubs. Together with its grounds, it was designed by Daniel Robertson for the Grogan family, who have owned the estate since Cromwellian times. There are three lakes within the ornamental grounds, the ruins of a tower house, a statue walk, a walled garden and hothouses; among the hundreds of species there is a huge rhododendron arboretum near the Castle.

Features: there is an Agricultural Museum in the estate farmyard, which has displays of rural transport and antique implements

Kilkenny Castle

Kilkenny Castle, National Historic Park, Kilkenny
City, Co Kilkenny, Ireland
Telephone: (056) 21450 **fax:** (056) 63488

Location: set in extensive parklands, the Castle
dominates the city of Kilkenny
Opening: times are subject to restoration work;
from April to May from 10.00am to 5.00pm,
June to September from 10.00am to 7.00pm,
October to March from Tuesday to Saturday
from 10.30am to 12.45pm and from 2.00 to
5.00pm, Sundays from 11.00am to 12.45pm and
from 2.00 to 5.00pm
History: there has been a castle on the site since
1172, when the Norman knight Richard de Clare
built a wooden tower on the rocky height overlooking the River Nore. The first stone castle was
built 20 years later by William Marshall, Earl of
Pembroke. This was a square castle with a tower
at each corner; three of these survive. For 550
years it has been the home of the Butler family,
Earls, Marquesses and Dukes of Ormond. It was
a remarkable family, resilient, politically astute,
and faithful to the Crown and to Ireland after its
fashion. In 1969, the Castle passed into State
care and the Castle and grounds are now a
National Historic Park.
Features: the Castle today provides an insight
into a society which effectively no longer exists.

Lismore Castle

Lismore Castle, Lismore, Co Waterford, Ireland
Telephone: (058) 54424

Location: in the town of Lismore, where the entrance to the gardens is situated
Opening: daily from 11 May to 11 September, except Saturday, from 1.45 to 4.45pm
History: Lismore means 'great fort' in Irish, and the original castle here was built by Prince John in 1185. The Bishops of Lismore built their palace on its ruins, and the estate was granted for a time to Sir Walter Raleigh for a rent of £12.00pa. Raleigh sold the property to Richard Boyle, later the first Earl of Cork, who rebuilt the Castle, parts of which are incorporated into the present structure, which was built in the mid-19th century by the sixth Duke of Devonshire. The first Earl of Cork also built the thick defensive walls in 1626, which still surround the upper garden. The upper garden is linked to the lower garden by the staircase to the Riding House, which was built in 1631. Lismore is now the Irish home of the Duke of Devonshire.
Features: fine collection of shrubs, including magnolias and camellias and an ancient yew walk

Malahide Castle

Malahide Castle, Malahide, Co Dublin, Ireland
Telephone: (01) 845 2655 **fax:** (01) 845 2528

Location: 14km (8.69 miles) NE of Dublin via Fairview and the Malahide road
Opening: daily from Monday to Friday from 10.00am to 5.00pm; November to March Saturdays, Sundays and bank holidays from 2.00 to 5.00pm; from April to October on Saturdays from 11.00am to 6.00pm and Sundays and bank holidays from 2.00 to 6.00pm, and open from 11.30am on Sundays May through September
History: the property was granted to Robert Talbot by Prince John, Lord of Ireland, in 1185 and the family lived there continuously until 1976, except for a brief period when they were evicted by Cromwell. The Castle boasts the only surviving original great hall, which is hung with an impressive collection of family portraits. It is said that 14 Talbot cousins breakfasted here before riding out to the Battle of the Boyne in 1690, never to return. The Castle's tiny doorway leads into this panelled oak room, where a Flemish carving of the Coronation of the Virgin hangs over the fireplace. It is said to have disappeared when the Talbots were banished, and mysteriously reappeared upon their return.
Features: a delightful demesne created since 1948, with many species of trees and shrubs

Ormond Castle

Ormond Castle, Carrick-on-Suir, Co Tipperary, Ireland
Telephone: (051) 40787

Location: NW of the port of Waterford, the Castle stands at a strategic point on the River Suir commanding access to Clonmel to the west
Opening: daily from mid-June to September from 9.30am to 6.30pm
History: built by the Butler family, the surviving buildings date from two periods on a site first inhabited by them in 1309 and subsequently given to, and re-purchased from, the Franciscans. The battlemented towers and some ruined remains linking them with the river on the south side of the site are all that survive from Sir Edmund MacRichard Butler's castle of the mid-15th century. The extensive manor buildings adjoining the towers and extending the Castle on the north side were built by Tomás Bubh (Black Tom) Butler, the tenth Earl of Ormond, over a century later. After Black Tom's death in 1614, his successors moved to Kilkenny Castle.
Features: in 1947, the Castle was placed in the care of the Commissioners of Public Works, who have carried out extensive renovation, restoring the manor house which was Black Tom's most important contribution to Irish architecture.

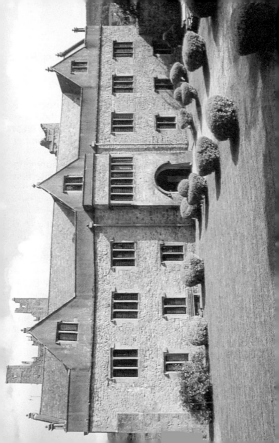

Parke's Castle

Parke's Castle, Fivemile Bourne, Co Leitrim,
Ireland
Telephone: (071) 64149

Location: situated on the Sligo-Dromahaire
road, beside Lough Gill
Opening: St Patrick's weekend and October
daily from 10.00am to 5.00pm; from 10 April to
end May from Tuesday to Sunday and on public
holidays from 10.00am to 5.00pm; from June to
September daily from 9.30am to 6.30pm
History: the stronghold of an important local
16th-century family, where in 1588, Sir Brian
O'Rorke sheltered Francisco de Cuellar, the
shipwrecked Spanish Armada officer. O'Rorke
was later indicted for high treason and executed
in London in 1591. During the 17th century,
Captain Robert Parke purchased the estate from
Con O'Rourke, including the strong castle with a
walled enclosure called a bawn, so typical of
early 17th-century Plantation settlements. The
manor house has three storeys conjoined to an
arched gate. The parapet walls are pierced with
musket loops and behind them is a raised wall-
walk.
Features: archaeological excavations revealed
the foundations of the bawn's 17th-century
structures, including a blacksmith's forge, a well
and a sallyport or watergate to the lake.

Slane Castle

Slane Castle, Slane, Co Meath, Ireland
Telephone: Irish Heritage Properties, Dublin (01) 285 9323

Location: 48km (32 miles) N of Dublin, on the main road to Londonderry; the Castle overlooks the River Boyne
Opening: at the time of writing the Castle had been extensively damaged by fire and was closed for restoration, but it will reopen on completion
History: the Castle dates from 1785, and was begun by the second Lord Conyngham and completed by his son, the first Marquess of Conyngham, husband of the Lady Conyngham who was mistress of King George IV. It was said of her that 'the vice queen has not a brain in her head only a hand to grab pearls and diamonds and a magnificent balcony to show them upon'. Portraits of the pair by Sir Thomas Lawrence hang in the magnificent Gothic ballroom, which has filigree vaulting by Thomas Hopper. It was built specially for the King's visit in 1821. This Gothic Revival castle was designed by James Wyatt and Francis Johnson.
Features: King George IV's writing desk, said to be one of the finest pieces of furniture in Ireland, can be seen in the drawing room.

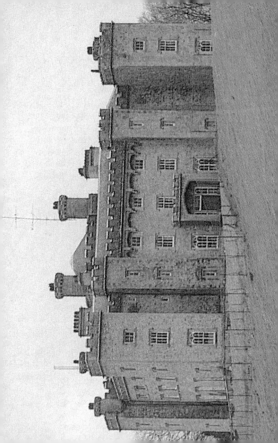

Tullynally Castle

Tullynally Castle, Castlepollard, Co Westmeath, Ireland
Telephone: (044) 61159

Location: 1.5km (1 mile) outside Castlepollard on the Granard road, 20km (13.5 miles) from Mullingar
Opening: gardens June to September daily from 10.00am to 6.00pm; Castle rooms from 15 July to 15 August daily from 2.00 to 6.00pm and at other times for groups by arrangement
History: an original 17th-century building, which was brought by Henry Pakenham in 1655, since when it has been the seat of the Pakenham family. The Gothic additions made by Francis Johnson for the second Lord Longford were part of a series of enlargements to the original building, which made Tullynally the largest castellated house in Ireland. Maria Edgeworth wrote in 1506 'Lord Longford has finished and furnished his castle and made such a comfortable nest that he must certainly get some bird with pretty plumage to fill it', a reference to Lady Georgina Lygon, who added informal gardens to the landscaped park and walled gardens.
Features: the house is a museum of 14th-century gadgets with splendid Victorian laundries and kitchens and a fine collection of portraits and furniture

Castel Beséno

Castel Beséno, Besanello, Province of Trento, Italy
Telephone: (0461) 233770

Location: a 20-minute walk from Besenello, on the right of the river and Verona-Bolzano road, halfway between Rovereto and Trento; shuttle bus service on Saturdays, Sundays and holidays
Opening: daily from 1 April to 30 October from 9.00am to 12 noon and from 2.30 to 5.30pm
History: this fortified and turreted Castle covers the entire hilltop, enabling it to control the road to the province of Vicenza. In all, it covers an area of 16,400m^2 (19,614.4sq yd), and is one of the largest castles on the southern side of the central Alps. The 15th-century fortifications resulting from the introduction of firearms remain as three majestic keeps and their small yards for cannon. The tournament field, the traps, and the elegant Filandèla loggia are proof of its eventful past. The two castle walls enclose the three medieval neuclei enfeoffed by the Lords of Beséno. After a feud of the Prince-Bishops at the beginning of the 14th century, the Castle was the property of the Castelbarco family, who kept it until the second half of the following century, when it was bought by the Trapp family.
Features: now beautifully restored, it belongs to the Province of Trento

Castello di Sabbionara d'Avio

Castello di Sabbionara d'Avio, Sabbionara d'Avio, Italy
Telephone: (0464) 64453

Location: on the Verona-Trento road, in the Valle dell'Adige, to the left of Ala and the Castle is the first one you reach
Opening: from Tuesday to Sunday from 1 February to 30 September from 10.00am to 1.00pm and from 2.00 to 6.00pm; from Thursday to Sunday from 1 October to 30 December from 10.00am to 1.00pm and from 2.00 to 5.00pm
History: Trento was already a regional capital at the time of the Prince-Bishops, and the historical road link to central Europe is guarded by many castles, especially in the Vallagarina, south of Trento. Sabbionara d'Avio perches on the sloping right bank of the River Adige, overlooking the town of Avio. The Castle was feuded over for several centuries by the Castelbario family, including William II who reputedly entertained Dante Alighieri; it has the unique architectural lines of a medieval alpine fortress, influenced by 13th-century Veronese culture.
Features: the Room of Love in the keep, and the Parade of Combatants in the guardroom; now the property of the Fund for the Italian Environment with the exception of the Picadóra Tower, retained by the Castelbarco heirs.

Blair Castle

Blair Castle, Blair Atholl, Pitlochry, Perthshire
PH18 5TL, Scotland
Telephone: (0796) 481207 **fax:** 481487

Location: 129km (80 miles) N of Edinburgh via
M90 motorway to Perth, then 56km (35 miles)
from Perth via A9; from the railway station at
Blair Atholl, there is a free minibus service to the
Castle
Opening: daily from 1 April to last Friday in
October from 10.00am to 6.00pm; last admissions one hour before closing
History: commanding a strategic position in the
central Scottish Highlands, Blair Castle has been
the home and fortress of the Earls and Dukes of
Atholl for over 700 years. It was the last castle to
be besieged in Great Britain during the Jacobite
uprising in 1746, and during its history has been
occupied by opposing forces on no less than
four occasions.
Features: now the home of the tenth Duke of
Atholl, who has the unique distinction of having
the only remaining private army in Europe, the
Atholl Highlanders. There are 32 rooms open to
the public, fully furnished with beautiful furniture and a fine collection of paintings, arms and
armor, china, costumes and treasures which present an insight into Scottish life between the
16th and 20th centuries.

Brodick Castle

Brodick Castle, Isle of Arran, Strathclyde KA27 8HY, Scotland
Telephone: (0770) 302202

Location: cross the Firth of Clyde by ferry from Ardrossan to Brodick; the Castle lies about 3km (2 miles) to the N of the town

Opening: daily from 1 to 18 April and from 2 May to 30 September; from 19 April to 1 May and from 2 to 23 October on Mondays, Wednesdays and Saturdays, from 1.00 to 5.00pm; last admissions at 4.30pm

History: Brodick Castle stands on a site fortified by the Vikings and in part dates from the 13th century, with extensions added in 1652 and 1844. It is the ancient seat of the Dukes of Hamilton and more recently the home of the late Mary, Duchess of Montrose. She started the woodland garden in 1923, which is now one of Europe's finest rhododendron gardens. The formal gardens date from 1710 and are restored as a Victorian garden.

Features: considerable variety of superb silver, porcelain and paintings from the collections of the Dukes of Hamilton, William Beckford and the Earls of Rochford, including sporting pictures and trophies. The Castle is now managed by the National Trust for Scotland. Car parking available, but access for the disabled is limited.

Brodie Castle

Brodie Castle, Brodie, Forres, Moray IV36 0TE,
Scotland
Telephone: (030) 94 371

Location: off the main A96 road between
Forres (7km/4.5 miles) and Nairn (14km/9
miles), at Brodie
Opening: from 1 April to 26 September from
Monday to Saturday from 11.00am to 6.00pm
and on Sundays from 2.00 to 6.00pm; from 2 to
17 October on Saturdays from 11.00am to
5.00pm and on Sundays from 2.00 to 5.00pm;
last admissions 45 minutes before closing
History: the Brodies are recorded as inhabiting
the area in the reign of Alexander III, but first
endowed with the land in 1160 by Malcolm IV.
Damaged in 1645 during the Montrose Cam-
paigns, the Castle is now based on a 16th-
century 'Z' plan with later additions in the 17th
and 19th centuries. The Castle, its contents and
70.82 ha (175 acres) were acquired from the
25th Brodie of Brodie and in 1980 transferred
into the National Trust for Scotland.
Features: fine French furniture; English, Continental and Chinese porcelain; paintings from
17th-century Dutch to 18th and early 19th-
century English watercolours and French
Impressionists; a 1.62ha (four acre) pond in the
grounds; nature trail and an observation hide.

Caerlaverock Castle

Caerlaverock Castle, Glencaple Road, Dumfries,
Dumfriesshire DG1 4RM, Scotland
Telephone: (038) 777 244

Location: 135km (84 miles) S of Glasgow and
19km (12 miles) S of Dumfries, from where the
Castle is signposted, on the B725 road
Opening: daily from 9.30 to 7.00pm from April
to September and from October to March closing three hours earlier; opening at 2.00pm on
Sundays throughout the year
History: constructed in the 1270s by Sir Her-
bert de Maxwell with a twin-towered gatehouse
and keep combined around the entrance. The
Castle is triangular in shape, tapering back in a
southerly direction from the gatehouse. Water-
filled moats surround the Castle, which was
reached by a pivoted swing bridge leading to an
entrance passage with iron-bound doors and a
portcullis. The original wooden galleries around
the walls were later replaced with stone. Much
of the present building dates from 1320, when
the Murdoch Tower was added, although there
were considerable extensions during the 15th
century. In 1634, Robert Maxwell, first Earl of
Nithsdale, constructed domestic accommodation within the south and east walls.
Features: a most beautiful castle, with a grand
stairway to the rooms on the eastern flank

Craigievar Castle

Craigievar Castle, Alford, Aberdeenshire AB33 8JF, Scotland.
Telephone: National Trust (031) 226 5922

Location: 40km (25 miles) W of Aberdeen via the B9119 and A980, this beautiful castle stands amid trees in a small park above Leochel Burn.
Opening: from 1 May to 30 September, from 2.00 to 6.00 pm, grounds from 9.30 am to sunset; groups by prior appointment, no coaches or disabled facilities.
History: the building was begun in the early 17th century by the Mortimer family, who by necessity sold it unfinished to William Forbes. Forbes completed the Castle in 1626. The lower two-thirds are in the form of a trio of harled towers with a single door and a minimum of windows. This provided the fortification above which, stepped out from the walls and running all round the structure, are gables, balustrades, coned turrets and chimney stacks. The castle house is of L-shaped design with a smaller tower between two larger ones.
Features: a wide granite stairway leading to the first floor hall, which is by far the grandest room, with its vaulted roof, huge fireplace, carved oak panelling and remarkable plasterwork on the ceiling, plus a gigantic coat of arms above the mantelpiece.

Culzean Castle

Culzean Castle, Maybole, Strathclyde KA19 8LE, Scotland
Telephone: (065) 56274

Location: 18km (12 miles) S of Ayr, on the A719 coast road and 6km (4 miles) W of Maybole on the B7023 and A719. The Castle stands in a fine cliff-top position.
Opening: daily from 1 April to 31 October from 10.30am to 5.30pm; last admissions 5.00pm
History: a Robert Adam castle, built between 1772 and 1790 for David, tenth Earl of Cassillis, Culzean consists of an older castle that has been incorporated within later additions. The original building was an L-shaped medieval tower, which was replaced in the 17th century by a fortified complex. The Castle has been associated with the Kennedy family since the late 14th century, until they, with the fifth Marquess of Ailsa, gave the Culzean castle and estate to the National Trust for Scotland.
Features: much of the interior design and furniture was designed by Robert Adam; most notable is the magnificent oval staircase and the Round Drawing Room on the first floor of the drum tower; also the Old Eating Room at the base of the original tower house. The Eisenhower Room traces the General's career, and his close association with Culzean.

Drum Castle

Drum Castle, Drumonk by Banchory, AB31 3EY,
Scotland
Telephone: (0330) 811204

Location: 15km (10 miles) W of Aberdeen, via
the A93 Perth road
Opening: daily from 1 May to 30 September
from 2.00 to 6.00pm, and from 3 to 25 April and
from 2 to 31 October on Saturdays and Sundays
from 2.00 to 5.00pm; last admissions 45 minutes
before closing
History: one of the three oldest tower houses in
Scotland. It was built in the late 13th century by
Richard Cementarius, the King's master mason
and first Provost of Aberdeen. Additions were
made in 1619 and during the reign of Queen Victoria to this Jacobean mansion house. In 1323
King Robert the Bruce gave a charter of the
Royal Forest of Drum to his faithful armor-bearer
William de Irwyn. The family connection
remained unbroken until the property was
bequeathed to the National Trust for Scotland in
1976 by the late Mr HQ Forbes Irvine.
Features: the fine Irvine Room, which contains
family memorabilia; the 40.47ha (100 acre) Old
Wood of Drum, a natural oak wood; arboretum;
garden of historic roses; woodland walks, car
park, play and picnic area; wheelchairs are welcome and made available.

Dunrobin Castle

Dunrobin Castle, Golspie, Sutherland KW10 6SF, Scotland
Telephone: (0408) 633177 **fax:** 633800

Location: 40km (25 miles) N of Inverness via the A9, 1.5km (1 mile) N of Golspie; the Castle overlooks the Dornoch Firth and North Sea
Opening: Monday to Thursday 10.30am to 12.30pm during May and 10.30am to 5.00pm from June to September; Sundays 1.00pm to 5.00pm
History: it is believed that a castle first stood on the site in the 11th century; certainly there was a keep there in 1275. The oldest part of the present building, which is the most northerly of Britain's great houses, dates from the early 15th century. In the middle of the 17th century, an L-shaped block was built opposite the medieval tower at Dunrobin to form a courtyard castle. In 1839, Sir Charles Barry designed the present building for the second Duke of Sutherland.
Features: a French-style château with tall tapering cones forms the contrasting southern façade, while other sides are dominated by two towers, one larger than the other. The interior comprises 189 rooms, which are adorned by priceless pieces of furniture and paintings by Canaletto, Romney, Reynolds and others. The ghost of Margaret Gordon frequents the attics.

Edinburgh Castle

Edinburgh Castle, Castle Rock, Royal Mile, Edinburgh, Scotland
Telephone: (031) 225 9846

Location: in the city center, easily accessible by public transport with parking nearby
Opening: daily from April to September from 9.30am to 5.05pm except Sundays, 11.00 to 5.05pm; from October to March from 9.30am to 4.20pm except on Sundays, 12.30 to 3.35pm
History: an occupied site since prehistoric times, with the oldest structure still standing St Margaret's Chapel, dating from the reign of David I (1124-1153). The fortress was demolished in 1313, and rebuilt by David II in 1357 as a tower house and a gatehouse linked by a curtain wall. The gatehouse was replaced in the 1570s by the Portcullis Gate or Argyll Tower. A barracks added in the Crown Square in 1755 was altered in the 1920s to create the Scottish National War Memorial. The Royal Palace, an extension of David II's Tower, was built by James I and modified by James IV, Queen Mary and James VI before being heightened with battlements in the 19th century.
Features: chamber where Mary, Queen of Scots, gave birth to James VI, James V's crown, James IV's sword and his Great Hall with beautiful hammerbeam roof.

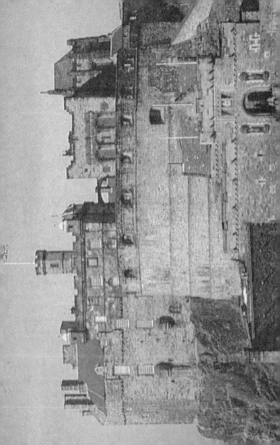

Floors Castle

Floors Castle, Roxburgh Estate Office, Kelso, Roxburghshire TD5 7SF, Scotland
Telephone: (0573) 223333 **fax:** 226056

Location: 70km (43.5 miles) SE of Edinburgh, the Castle is clearly signposted 2km (1.25 miles) from the town of Kelso; it is flanked by the River Tweed and overlooks extensive parklands
Opening: daily in July and August from 10.30am to 5.30pm, last admissions 45 minutes before closing; from 25 April to end June and in September, open Sunday to Thursday plus Easter weekend and Sundays and Wednesdays in October from 10.30am to 4.00pm
History: designed by William Adam for the first Duke of Roxburghe, the building was started in 1721. In 1835, the sixth Duke commissioned WH Playfair to transform Floors, which he did by adding large east and west wings which also extend north, forming a partially enclosed court. To the south, a large covered *port-cochère* (porch) was added. Externally, the Castle, with its multitude of spires and domes, has not changed since, although internally several rooms including the ballroom and dining room were remodelled at the turn of the century.
Features: 18th-century French furniture and magnificent tapestries

Fyvie Castle

Fyvie Castle, Fyvie, Grampian Region, Scotland
Telephone: (0651) 891263

Location: 38km (24 miles) N of Aberdeen via the A947, clearly signposted, the Castle lies to the right of the road 13km (8 miles) beyond Old Meldrum. Public transport is very limited
Opening: May to September from 11.00am to 6.00pm and Saturdays and Sundays during October from 2.00 to 4.00pm
History: site of a large medieval castle with walls 2.5m (98in) thick, and 8m (26ft 3in) high, this royal stronghold passed into the hands of Sir James de Linsay in 1380. The Castle forms a figure 2, with medieval walls forming the base and upright; the upper part, Leith Tower, was added in the 19th century. The Castle was transformed by Lord Fyvie, the first Earl of Dunfermline, and Chancellor of Scotland in 1601. This includes the celebrated southern façade, which joined the Edwardian gatehouse and the linking curtain wall to the eastern and western towers. At the end of the 17th century, the Castle fell into disrepair before being purchased by William Gordon. A new northern tower was built and the surrounding marshes drained.
Features: beautiful plasterwork and panelling, armor and weaponry and the Green Lady ghost.

Glamis Castle

Glamis Castle, Glamis, by Forfar, Angus DD8 1RQ, Scotland
Telephone: (0307) 84242 **fax:** (0307) 84257

Location: 19km (12 miles) N of Dundee, just off the A928, 1.5km (1 mile) N of Glamis
Opening: from 4 April to 11 October from 10.30am to 5.30pm, last admissions 45 minutes before closing; in the winter months, visitors are welcome by appointment with the administrator
History: a stone tower is thought to have existed on the site when it came into the possession of Sir John Lyon at the end of the 14th century. The Castle is dominated by an L-shaped tower house which lies at the heart of the building, with its 2.5m (98.5in) thick walls. The tower was raised and embellished with cone-capped turrets by the ninth Lord Glamis and first Earl of Kinghorn at the beginning of the 17th century. The Castle fell into ruin, but was meticulously rebuilt by the third Earl, leaving the Castle much as we see it today, although the west wing was destroyed by fire in the early part of the 19th century and rebuilt with a flat roof.
Features: the birthplace of Princess Margaret and legendary setting of Shakespeare's *Macbeth*; 'Glamis thou art...and yet would'st wrongly win thou'st have great Glamis...'. The interior is stacked with treasures and souvenirs.

Inveraray Castle

Inveraray Castle, Inveraray, Strathclyde, Scotland

Telephone: (0499) 2203 **fax:** (0499) 2421

Location: 60km (37 miles) NW of Glasgow via the A82 and A83

Opening: from April to October from 10.00am to 6.00pm except Sundays, opening at 1.00pm and closed on Fridays except during July and August; also closed from 1.00 to 2.00pm during April, May, September and October

History: the home of the Dukes of Argyll and headquarters of the Campbell clan. The Castle and the small town, which lie along the banks of Loch Fyne, were the brainchild of the third Duke, Archibald Campbell, and were first built in the middle of the 18th century. An original concept by Vanbrugh, the Castle as seen today is primarily the work of Roger Morris, who was assisted by William Adam and his sons John and Robert. The classic interior was arranged by Robert Mylne. The Castle is rectangular in shape.

Features: State Dining Room with painted wall panels and Robert Adam-designed ceiling; the very elaborate Tapestry Drawing Room with Beauvais tapestries, and Armoury Hall; paintings and extensive collection of Oriental and European porcelain arranged in cabinets within a China Turret

Stirling Castle

Stirling Castle, Stirling, SK18 1EJ, Scotland
Telephone: (0786) 462517 (shop) **fax:** Historic Scotland (0786) 464678 or telephone (0786) 450000

Location: 37km (23 miles) W of Edinburgh, via the M9 motorway, the Castle sits high on a rock
Opening: daily from 9.30am to 5.15pm, but closing at 4.20pm from October to March; on Sundays from 10.00am to 4.45pm and from October to March 12.30 to 3.35pm
History: it is believed that probably a prehistoric fort stood here originally, and that Stirling was probably the seventh-century city of Ludeu. The oldest part of the existing castle, contained within the north gate, dates from 1381, but constant and considerable changes have been wrought upon this strategic stronghold. The Stewart palace stood at the center of the castle and comprised four buildings built over some 150 years, destroyed by fire in the middle of the last century. The new building bears little resemblance to the original. The Castle was held by the English until the Battle of Bannockburn in 1314.
Features: the great hall, a fine late-medieval structure now lovingly restored; the carved wooden 'Stirling Heads', on the ceiling of the Royal Presence Chamber, and the Upper Square, with the Palace and Chapel Royal

Thirlestane Castle

Thirlestane Castle, Lauder, Berwickshire TD2 6RU, Scotland
Telephone: (0578) 722430 **fax:** 722761

Location: 45km (28 miles) S of Edinburgh via the A68 to Lauder, from which the Castle is clearly signposted
Opening: from Sunday to Friday in July and August from 2.00 to 5.00pm, last admissions 30 minutes before closing; also Wednesday, Thursday and Sunday in May and September, and Easter
History: the present Castle, home of the Maitlands whose ancestry can be traced back to 1066, was not built until the late 16th century by John, the first Lord Maitland and it replaced Old Thirlestane Castle, a medieval L-shaped tower house. Fort Lauder had originally occupied the site, erected by Edward I and rebuilt by Edward II in 1324. Sited on a rocky crag overlooking Leader Water, it underwent extensive rebuilding and re-landscaping in both the 17th and 19th centuries, when the front was stretched to include two new pavilions and square turrets with conical roofs were added.
Features: fine plasterwork ceilings from the Restoration; remarkable collection of family portraits; large collection of historic toys, and a Border Country Life Museum.

Alcázar

Parador de Zafra, Plaza Corázon de Maria 7,
06300 Zafra (Badajoz), Spain
Telephone: (924) 554540 **fax:** (924) 551018

Location: 77km (50 miles) SE of Badajoz via
the N432 road, and 135km (90 miles) N of
Sevilla via the N630, in the center of Zafra
Opening: the four-star Parador, which operates
as the Hotel Hernán Cortés, is open every day
History: this fortified palace is one of the most
beautiful in Extremadura, and was the home of
the conquistador Hernán Cortés before he left
for the New World. Construction began in 1437
and was completed in 1443 under the direction
of Don Lorenzo Suàrez de Figueroa, and it is his
coat of arms that appears on the façade, interior
decorations and coffered ceilings, together with
the coat of arms of his wife, Maria Manuela. The
Castle commanded two important mountain
passes on the road from Jerez de los Caballeros
to Fregenal de la Sierra. Built over an old Arab
castle, the splendors of the past have been
retained in the Parador of Zafra for those in quest
of enjoyment.
Features: 38km (25 miles) away is the city of
Jerez de los Caballeros, surrounded by ramparts
and also crowned by a castle filled with a variety
of art treasures

Castell de Ducs de Cardona

Parador de Turismo Ducs de Cardona, 08261 Cardona (Barcelona), Spain
Telephone: (93) 869 1275 **fax:** 869 1636

Location: 100km (65 miles) NW of Barcelona via the motorway to its end N of Manresa, then via Santpedor to Cardona; the Castle stands just 120m (131yds) NE of the fortified city
Opening: the four star Parador has a restaurant and 60 rooms, and is open every day
History: the most important fortress in Catalonia, both because of its size, and because of the great influence of the Castle and its feudal lords in the history of Catalonia. From the beginning of the ninth century, the Castle has belonged to the family of the Admiral and High Constable of Aragón, Don Ramón Folch, Duke of Cardona. Its walled enclosure contains the Church of San Vicente, consecrated in 1040; it is one of the most uniform romanesque constructions, and a national monument. San Ramón Nonato, a member of the Cardona family, died at the Castle in 1240, bringing about a miracle of the Eucharist. The Chapel of St Ramón Nonato is said to have been built on the same place where the saint died after the viaticum from Jesus Christ.
Features: the church crypt, mausoleum and romanesque gratings, the second-century castle tower known as Minyona and its famous keep

Castle of Olité

Parador de Olité, Plaza de los Teobaldos 2,
31390 Olité (Navarra), Spain
Telephone: (948) 740000 (Parador); 740035
(Castle) **fax:** (948) 740201

Location: 42km (28 miles) S of Pamplona via
the N121 road to Zaragoza
Opening: daily except on Sunday afternoons
from 1 June to 30 September from 10.00am to
2.00pm and from 4.00 to 5.00pm
History: this royal palace, one of the most
Gothic civil works in Europe, was built on the
site of the Roman praesidium. Modified several
times, the Castle frequently lodged the
Navarrese kings during the 13th and 14th centuries, but most notably Charles III of Navarre
(1387-1425) restored the Old Palace and built
its large towers, still surviving today. The picturesque complexity of its plan has no equal among
other buildings of its type. A diverse and secret-
ive castle, Olité is said to have had as many
rooms as there are days in the year, all linked by
countless galleries and winding stairs, each
more sumptuous than the one before.
Features: well-preserved fortified precinct
from the first century AD; underground passages
and galleries with hidden exits and secret doors;
remains of the lions' den (a ditch with thick
walls) at the foot of the 'Las Atalayas' tower

Beaumaris Castle

Beaumaris Castle, Beaumaris, Gwynedd LL58
8AP, Wales
Telephone: (0248) 810361

Location: crossing the Menai bridge from
Bangor to Anglesey, Beaumaris is 6km (4 miles)
NE along the A545 E of the town center
Opening: daily from 9.30am to 6.30pm until 24
October; then daily from 9.30am to 4.00pm
except Sundays, from 2.00 to 4.00pm
History: begun in 1295, it was the last and the
largest of King Edward I's Welsh castles.
Designed by Master James of St George, Beaumaris is regarded as the ultimate in symmetrical
concentric design. Surrounded by a water-filled
moat and with its own protected access to the
sea, it had its own medieval docks capable of
handling ships of 40 tonnes (88,184lb). The
concentric castle, with one high ring of defense
inside a lower one, was first perfected at Caer-
philly in 1268, and had advantages of economy,
unity and compactness over the older keep and
bailey castle system. It also afforded a tremendous increase in fire power with the second line
of defenses able to fire over the outer walls.
Features: a 5.5m (18ft) moat, which originally
encircled the castle; an octagonal outer curtain
wall with 16 towers; unhappily, Beaumaris was
never completed owing to lack of finances.

Bodelwyddan Castle

Bodelwyddan Castle, New St Asaph, Clwyd
LL18 5YA, Wales
Telephone: (0745) 584060

Location: 50km (31 miles) W of Liverpool via
the M53 motorway and A55, opposite Marble
Church
Opening: daily except Fridays from Easter to
end October, from 10.00am to 5.00pm; last
admission 4.00pm; also on Fridays during July
and August
History: a house has stood on this site since
1460, and was purchased by Sir William Williams, Speaker of the English House of Com-
mons in 1680. The Castle underwent extensive
alterations under the first baronet of Bodelwyddan at the beginning of the 19th century,
with the present gothic appearance being the
result of work carried out by his son, Sir John
Hay-Williams, in the 1830s when the towers
were created and the battlements added to the
parapet. In 1982, the Castle was acquired by
Clwyd County Council. In partnership with the
National Portrait Gallery, it has redecorated and
refurbished the principal rooms, which now
make up the Williams Hall.
Features: much furniture on loan from the Victoria and Albert Museum; important collection
of 19th-century portraits

Caernarfon Castle

Caernarfon Castle, Castle Ditch, Caernarfon, Gwynedd LL55 2AY, Wales
Telephone: (0286) 677617

Location: to the W of Caernarfon town, overlooking the Menai Strait
Opening: daily from 9.30am to 6.30pm until 24 October; then daily from 9.30am to 4.00pm except Sundays, from 2.00 to 4.00pm
History: built mostly between 1283 and 1292. A fortress palace, it was designed as the new seat of government for North Wales, and was the birthplace of Edward II in 1284. Caernarfon withstood the assaults of Owain Glyndwr, defended by only 28 men, but was surrendered in the Civil War. The Castle was extensively restored in Victorian and later times, and was the site of the ceremonial investiture of Prince Charles as the Prince of Wales in July 1969. The Castle has been owned continuously by the Crown, and is the nearest building Wales has to a royal palace. Its plan, however, is unusual, being shaped rather like an hourglass which was originally divided by a crosswall at the narrowest part into two wards. The earthen mound of an earlier Norman motte and bailey castle, built in 1090 by Earl Hugh of Chester, occupies most of the upper ward.
Features: museum of the Royal Welch Fusiliers

Harlech Castle

Harlech Castle, Harlech, Gwynedd LL46 2YH
Telephone: (0766) 780552

Location: Harlech stands on a high outcrop of rock beside the A496 coast road, 18km (12 miles) N of Barmouth

Opening: daily from 9.30am to 6.30pm until 24 October; then daily from 9.30am to 4.00pm except Sundays, and on Sundays from 2.00 to 4.00pm

History: built between 1283 and 1289. Standing some 60m (200ft) above the old sea level, even today the Castle's inner walls and towers stand almost to their full height. Designed by Master James of St George, who became its constable in 1290, it is very much a concentric castle, combining defensive fortification perfectly blended with accommodation. Harlech was captured by Owain Glyndwr in 1404, who held his parliaments there and reputedly crowned himself Prince of Wales. During the Wars of the Roses, it was held for the Lancastrians by the Welsh constable. Surrendering after a long seige, it was the last to fall to Parliament, immortalized in the song *Men of Harlech*.

Features: a splendid gatehouse with its vaulted ceiling and defended stairway to the sea, gated and heavily fortified, dropping down the west side of the Castle, almost the full 60m (200ft)

Glossary

Aisled: divided into three parts longitudinally by two arcades supporting the roof

Allure: the wall-walk which runs behind the battlements

Apse: the rounded east wall of a church or chapel

Arcade: a row of arches; when applied to a wall and used for decorative purposes, **blind arcade**

Archère: a loop-hole

Bailey: or **ward**, the courtyard of a castle which is defended

Ballista: an engine worked by tension and used for throwing projectiles

Barbican: a small advanced fortification used to protect a gateway

Barmkin: another word for **bailey**, used in connection with pele towers

Bartizan: or **eschaugette**, a turret that projects from the top of a wall or tower

Bastide: military settlement laid out along Roman lines in southern France in the 14th century

Batter: an inward slope to a wall face

Belfry: or **beffroi**, a seige tower

Berm: ledge sited at the base of a wall to stop debris falling into a moat or wet ditch

Brattice: or **bretèche**, a movable wooden structure or tower, usually used to defend the end of a bridge

Burgh: Anglo-Saxon fortified township

Casemate: gallery built outside the base of a wall, fitted with loop-holes through which archers could fire; also used for a vaulted chamber in the base of a tower from which flanking fire could be directed

Castellan: or **constable**, the commander of a castle, or the official in charge in the absence of its owner

Cat: popular name for a **penthouse**, a movable shelter for miners and rams; this is also known as a **sow** or **mouse**

Chamber: a private room

Chemise: a wall built closely around a **donjon**

Constable: *see* **castellan**

Corbel: a projecting stone that acts as a support for a beam; several tiers of corbels may be used to carry a parapet or tower

Coursière: the wooden roofing erected over a wall-walk

Crenel: or **crenelle**, one of the gaps or square notches between the raised parts in the castell-

Château de Chaumont was built on the ruins of a tenth century fortress founded by Eudes I, Count of Blois. The south-east façade illustrated of the 15th century Château still has a most impressive drawbridge between the two circular gatehouse

towers

ation of a battlement

Curtain: or **courtine**, the proper name for a length of wall linking two towers

Donjon: medieval word of French origins for a keep

Embrasure: a space hollowed into a thick wall, which allows the archer to stand closer to a loop

Enceinte: the complete circuit of walls and towers around a fortified place

Escalade: the assault of a castle made by climbing its walls

Eschaugette: *see* **bartizan**

Fausse braye: a line of defence along the floor of a ditch at the base of the walls

Forebuilding: a building projecting from the face of a keep, containing the entrance stair

Garderobe: latrine

Hall: a formal reception room used for the holding of courts and the entertaining of guests

Hoard: or **hourd**, an overhanging wooden gallery projecting from the parapet which enables the defenders to drop things on those below

Jamb: the side of a door or window; also in Scotland, the projecting wing of a tower house

Keep: the main tower of a castle, the strongest part and last resort, often isolated and capable of independent defense

Château d'Amboise, with its row of magnificent gable windows studded with carved pinnacles

184

Lintel: top piece of a door or window opening

List: interval between two lines of concentric walls

Loop: a narrow opening in a wall through which the defenders can discharge their arrows, and later, gunshot

Machicolation: a stone version of a hoard

Mangonel: an engine worked by torsion and used for throwing projectiles

Manlet: mobile screen which gives protective cover to besiegers

Merlon: the short solid part of a parapet between two crenelles

Meurtrière: hole over a passageway for dropping things on those below

Motte: a steep, large, artificial or natural mound of earth for the support of a timber tower

Mouse: *see* **cat**

Oratory: a small private chamber for prayer

Palisade: a fence of wooden stakes

Parados: a stone breastwork comprising crenelles and merlons on top that protects the rear of a sentry-walk; generally referred to as battlements

Parapet: like a **parados** but protecting the front of a sentry-walk

Penthouse: *see* **cat**

Pilaster: a flat, decorative buttress, often found on keeps

Piscina: a stone basin in a chapel, used for rinsing sacred vessels

Portcullis: wooden grille that slides vertically in grooves cut into the stonework of a gate passage

Postern: small exit gate or sallyport

Putlog holes: holes left by the withdrawal of timbers used to secure the scaffolding

Ravelin: a triangular-shaped outwork, sited in a ditch in front of a curtain wall

Sedilia: a row of stone seats set against the south wall of a chapel

Slighting: the deliberate destruction of a castle to prevent further use

Solar: private room used by the lord or his family

Sow: *see* **cat**

Talus: sloping wall, which is thicker at its base

Trèbuchet: a siege engine worked by counterpoise

Vault: an arched stone roof; a **barrel vault** has a semi-circular arch, and a **Gothic vault** has a pointed arch

Vice: a spiral staircase built into the thickness of the wall

Window seat: a stone seat built into the jamb of a window

Ward: *see* **bailey**

Yett: an iron gate found in tower houses

Index

Tamworth's sandstone walls
190 *probably date from the 1180s*